IN
SEARCH
OF
MYSELF:
LIFE, DEATH,
AND
PERSONAL
IDENTITY

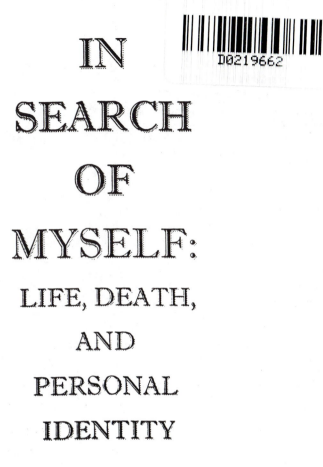

DANIEL KOLAK
William Paterson University of New Jersey

Wadsworth Publishing Company
I(T)P® An International Thomson Publishing Company

Belmont, CA • Albany, NY • Boston • Cincinnati • Johannesburg • London • Madrid • Melbourne
Mexico City • New York • Pacific Grove, CA • Scottsdale, AZ • Singapore • Tokyo • Toronto

Philosophy Editor: Peter Adams
Assistant Editor: Kerri Abdinoor
Editorial Assistant: Mindy Newfarmer
Marketing Manager: Dave Garrison
Print Buyer: Stacey Weinberger
Permissions Editor: Robert Kauser
Cover Design: Brian Day
Cover Image: Rene Magritte: *The Blank Signature*, Collection of Mr. and Mrs.
    Paul Mellon, National Gallery of Art
Printer: Webcom Ltd.

Printed in Canada
1 2 3 4 5 6 7 8 9 10

For more information, contact Wadsworth Publishing Company, 10 Davis Drive,
Belmont, CA 94002, or electronically at http://www.wadsworth.com

International Thomson Publishing Europe
Berkshire House
168-173 High Holborn
London, WC1V 7AA, United Kingdom

International Thomson Editores
Seneca, 53
Colonia Polanco
11560 México D.F. México

Nelson ITP, Australia
102 Dodds Street
South Melbourne
Victoria 3205 Australia

International Thomson Publishing Asia
60 Albert Street
#15-01 Albert Complex
Singapore 189969

Nelson Canada
1120 Birchmount Road
Scarborough, Ontario
Canada M1K 5G4

International Thomson Publishing Japan
Hirakawa-cho Kyowa Building, 3F
2-2-1 Hirakawa-cho, Chiyoda-ku
Tokyo 102 Japan

International Thomson Publishing Southern Africa
Building 18, Constantia Square
138 Sixteenth Road, P.O. Box 2459
Halfway House, 1685 South Africa

ISBN 0-534-23928-5

this book is dedicated to

Wendy Zentz Kolak

the woman of my dreams

By the same author:

Wisdom Without Answers
The Experience of Philosophy
Self & Identity
Self, Cosmos, God
Lovers of Wisdom
From Plato to Wittgenstein
One Thousand and One Questions
In Search of God: The Language and Logic of Belief
From the Presocratics to the Present: A Personal Odyssey
The Mayfield Anthology of Western Philosophy
Wittgenstein's Tractatus
Philosophy of Religion
Philosophy of Mind
Philosophy of Language
Philosophical Bridges

CONTENTS

Foreword

This is a wonderful and unusual book. It is a novel in which the characters do, and literally, are, philosophy. To read this novel is to live philosophy for a while.

The book does not attempt to describe philosophy or even to describe doing it, but it *does* philosophy. It captures your imagination and interest. It makes you do philosophy through the novel form. It entices you to do a special kind of philosophy. This kind of philosophy is abstract, respectful of the need for arguments, distinctions and clarity but without at all being remote and dry. On the contrary, it is intensely personal.

This book is very appropriate for Introduction to Philosophy courses, because its prime virtue is that it directly engages you in a philosophical wrestle. Because the wrestle to understand is so personal, it should appeal to many different kinds of introductory courses in philosophy: contemporary and historical, East and West, analytic and continental, mystical and literary. But it can and should be read both by the general reader and the philosopher: anyone wishing to wake up from the slumbers of commonsense will find it indispensable.

There is no other book quite like this one. It is in a superficial sense similar to John Perry's *A Dialogue Concerning Personal Identity and Immortality*; the similarity is with respect to some of the themes, but Kolak's book is much more engaging and entertaining. It has a plot. It will challenge readers. It is a novel which does philosophy. So this means it would appeal to teachers who would like to use literary texts as a part of their philosophy course. At the same time as having the advantages of the novel, they would not have to put up with the usual shortcomings: novels or short stories rarely contain arguments for and against positions; very seldom do novels directly concern philosophical themes. In that respect it has something in common with Jostein Gaarder's *Sophie's World*. But Kolak's world is deeper and more profound.

This book is delightful and fun. I enjoyed it very much. It has many moods. Sometimes it is deadly earnest, funny and silly, complex, irreverent. It is often Kafka-like, except more disturbing. Kafka, unlike Kolak, had the luxury of knowing who he was.

Garrett Thomson
The College of Wooster

WHO
AM
I?

I too am untranslatable.

Walt Whitman

I AM A BOOK.

I do not know that I exist. I am not conscious. I am not wise. I have neither a life, nor will I die. I have no goals, desires, or fears.

But I do have an identity: I am this book and not some other. And I have a purpose. To enlighten you: to existence, to yourself, to philosophy.

Perhaps you have read many books, perhaps only just a few. It does not matter. I was written neither for the learned nor for the unlearned. I was written just for you.

I know nothing about you. Yet I am all about you. And though you may need me to find out who you are I need you even more. I need you to exist.

WHO ARE YOU?

The lord whose is the oracle at Delphi neither reveals nor hides but gives tokens.

Heraclitus

MT. PARNASSUS: I'M WALKING ALONG THE steep lower slope. Above me the Phaedriades ("shining rocks") glint against the cloudless, azure sky. Stretching southward across the valley a pearly turquoise Plistus river winds to an ash blue jagged horizon: Mt. Cirphis and the Gulf of Corinth. Below me stand the ruins of the ancient theater and temple of Delphi, the seat of the oracle of Apollo, a place the ancient Greeks considered the center of the world.

According to legend, Zeus released two eagles into the

1

sky. One from the east, the other from the west, they flew toward the center until they met at Delphi at a spot marked in the temple by a stone called *omphalos*, the navel of the world. I sit on the burning rock. Except for the distant chorus of the cicadas all is absolutely still and quiet.

I am alone. Without wind the heat is oppressive. I take a sip of cool water from my canteen and wipe my brow. Every now and then the cicadas stop and the silence is like an explosion.

An ancient sanctuary. Before me looms the temple of Apollo with its empty altar. My eyes trace along what once were 15 two-story columns along either side and 6 across each front to the small antechamber where nearly three thousand years ago a beautiful and wise woman bearing the title "oracle," the official voice of God, declared Socrates to be the wisest because he claimed to know nothing except how little he knew. The story, often used as the starting point of philosophy, is notably absent from the sculpted rocks, the surrounding mountain, the valley; it remembers itself sleepily within me. Neither her name nor his, nor their likenesses, appear anywhere. It makes me smile to realize that this place and I are inextricably linked. Without me there is no story. The place needs me to tell its story and I need it to help me to know . . . to discover, to remember, to decide . . . who I am.

The only human figures appear along a small temple-like building, with caryatids instead of columns, carved in beautifully preserved metopes depicting the adventures of Theseus and Heracles. I think of the labyrinth and Ariadne, of the 12 Labors of that first son of God. Along with a hymn

2

to Apollo, accompanied by musical notation, scratched into that wall by unknown hands over three millennia ago, there is a message to us. To you and to me.

The ancient inscription is well known. Socrates, who wrote nothing, declared it to be his one and only dictum, what he lived by and what he died by. Two words. Unlike the images which come to this place through the memory that has somehow wound its way here through me, the ancient message needs no story and no storyteller. The writing is on the wall, literally, preserved for anyone who happens to follow this tortuous path through the cleft between these rocks:

"Know Yourself."

I get up and walk to the wall. Standing in the crisp, dark shadow I run my fingers along the Greek letters. I say the words aloud: *"gnothi s'afton." Know yourself.* I close my eyes and breathe in an invisible hive of energy, the air throbbing from the carmine-winged grasshoppers, the locusts, the thousand buzzing insects who even in their collective unities cannot find a common beat, though their songs remain the same.

Here, in this sacred place, there is no philosophy. The sun obliterates it, the air you breathe extinguishes it, the ten thousand nights of learned study vanish in the windless, thirsty heat. It took thousands of years for the treasures that once lined every corner of this place to vanish, for the ceilings to fall, the walls to crumble; all your theories and your thoughts vanish in an instant.

You open your eyes and now you are empty of your deeds, your degrees, your sweet pedantries. There is just this place, this remarkable, incredible place that once was Greece. And here you are, all alone, face to face with two words left over from what once was the center of the world:

Know Yourself.

ONE

DESCARTES AMONG THE RUINS

I know that I exist, and I inquire what I am, I whom I know to exist.

René Descartes

NIGHTFALL. I RETRIEVE MY BACKPACK from the *tholos*, a round building of unknown purpose, and make my way back along the colonnade into the temple. I will sleep in the antechamber where the Oracle once made her pronouncements. I take out my blanket and unroll it next to the back wall.

Above me the sky turns iridescent; a new crescent moon peeks at me over the edge of the ruin. The cicadas have not stopped but a new chorus of night locusts joins their tumult. A salamander scuttles into a crevice in the wall. I hear treefrogs. Lying on my back, staring up into the firmament, I try to sleep. It is too early, the stars too many and too bright; I cannot. The stillness sizzles. The darkness is full of everything.

Moonrise. The silver light swallows the stars and returns them to the sky undigested. The temple and I lie silently beneath the chiaroscuro spectacle, afloat in a sea of insect sound. A sweet saffronlike smell of flowers wallows in the warm evening breeze.

I feel strangely restless in my tired calm. A night bird, high overhead, croaks primevally in the stars. The crickets chirp. A single black cloud, thin as a razor, races across the face of the moon.

Suddenly I heard a sound echo faintly from the steep hillside. It came again, louder. A primitive timbre. An ancient instrument? I sat up. Again that sound. I stood up and looked over the side wall: ash-lilac mountains, cypress trees, moonshadows; a strange, crepuscular light. A hornpipe? When again I turned to look I saw a woman sitting up on the high wall, a majestic and beautiful figure in a flowing robe. Her skin glowed marboreally against the sky, a translucent silhouette beneath the crescent moon. Across her breasts the Greek letters Π and Θ were sewn into the tightly threaded fabric, one above the other, with degrees marked between them like the rungs of a ladder. In her right hand she held books; in her left, a scepter.

"Who are you? How did you get up there!"

Her eyes locked on me. I had never been looked at like that before, at least not by a human being. By an insect or animal, perhaps, poised and predatory, single minded, reptilian.

"You do not recognize me?"

Atop her flows of long black hair I caught a glint of golden laurel leaves.

"You are Philosophy," I said. "The Goddess of Wisdom, the one who consoled Boethius before his death." I smiled. "Except you don't exist."

"Why not?"

"Because I do."

"How do you know?"

"I think, therefore I am," I laughed.

"Oh, René," she cooed seductively, "I too can think."

I shook my head. "I think, therefore you do not."

"How do you know that?"

"Because this is a dream."

She put down the books and scepter. "You've come to the right place." With the slightest tilt forward she glided down off the high wall, in slow motion, a wingless bird. "What makes you think this is a dream?"

"You flew! You just flew!"

"Ah. So you reason thus: I see a goddess fly, therefore, I must be dreaming?"

"I know Goddesses do not exist. Therefore I reason, correctly, that I am dreaming a most extraordinary dream, that I converse with an apparition, a figment of my imagination."

"Do I look like a figment of your imagination?"

"Not at all." Staring into her fiery eyes I felt an eerie presence. How strange to look at eyes and believe they are not eyes, that there is no one there behind them. Behind my own eyes I wondered: what eyes am I seeing her with? "I admit I am dumbfounded. Doubly so. A realistic and lucid dream such as this, in which I find myself experiencing apparitions with the clearness and distinctness of waking life disturbs me exactly the way in waking life I should fear for my sanity were experience suddenly to turn tenuous, disjointed, discontinuous--"

"Tell me, then, who wrote these words:

> I perceive so clearly that there exist no certain marks by which the state of waking can ever be distinguished from sleep, that I feel greatly astonished; and in amazement I almost persuade myself that I am now dreaming."[1]

I smiled. "The words are mine."

She smiled back. "Well, then?"

"I was making a philosophical point. Except for extraordinary cases such as this, dreams usually are less vivid, they lack continuity, they are not as bright--"

"But think, my dear René, think: if objects in dreams appeared to you as such you would not run from them, engage with them, talk with them. You would instead say: look at those insubstantial images! How could you be deceived by something that announces itself as an appearance and says, outright, 'I am a deception?' That you ever are deceived should thus alert you to this deep and fundamental truth."

"What - that I can't distinguish dream from reality?"

"That even the most distinguished philosopher deceives himself with the distinction."

"Between dream and reality?"

"As surely as between himself and others."

What a bizarre and amusing twist, I thought, in one move to thus challenge within myself the distinction between dream and reality and between self and other; in waking life I had gone the other way around in two moves to find what I had thought was absolute certainty. But perhaps I had succeeded only with the intellect. Did not the very fact of this dream suggest hidden doubts still lingered deep within my soul?[2]

"I will wake up and you will disappear," I said. "That's the difference between you and me, between dream and reality. You don't exist in the real world."

"What world is that?"

"The world outside my mind."

"You know any such world, René? How! By what experience?"

"Not by experience. By reason."

"Ah. By reason you mean by argument, by which you mean by strings of sentences, by which you mean by strings of words? Then by what you know you must mean not world but theory. For that is to what your words connect you: not to the world in which your being is inscribed but to descriptions, narratives, a story."

"The real world is not a story."

"The real world does not exist, except in stories."

"That's what this is."

9

"Is that what you think?"

"In a matter of speaking, yes."

"In a manner of speaking?" She laughed. "What about the manner of experiencing? Is this a story you are telling yourself, in which a description of Descartes encounters a description of Philosophy?"

"No," I said.

"No? Just like that: no? No! This, my dear and imaginary friend, is not a story but a world that you are in."

"This world is a dream."

"Know you any other world, or any other self, as such?"

"Tell me what you mean by *world*," I said. "Impress me with mathematics, not poetry."

"By mathematics you mean nonsense?"

"I'd like to understand."[3]

"A world," said Philosophy, "is an outside with an inside. Unlike a story, description, or theory, a world consists in space and time conjoined by two essential aspects: object and subject, such that without either there can be neither, and no world as such."[4]

"You mean, a world must be described from—"

"No, no; experienced from."

"All right, yes," I said, "experienced from the first-person point of view. That's why this what I call *dream* you call *world*?"[5]

She nodded. "You are - or, I should say," she pointed at me, "'that' is - the world's subject. Whereas these walls," she gestured at the ruins, "the colonnade, the sky, even, from your point of view, me - are its objects. Subject and object are two aspects of one and the same being. And that being is the world."

"Because this is a dream," I said, "I can understand that. Dream objects exist only in my mind. But the real temple of Delphi – not this one I see here in the dream but the temple made of stone – has existed for centuries outside my mind–"

"Does the stone make the temple real? Or is mind the temple?"

"I don't understand."

"Does the 'real' temple - the one you just described as 'existing outside your mind' - exist as an object?"

"Yes."

"No, René!"

"Why?"

"Because what does *object* mean? Does *object* not require the notion of *subject?*"

"Not in the real world, no: real objects require no subject to exist. There is no *I* involved in the existence of objects in the real world, they exist regardless of whether I perceive them."

"Look at your conception: 'the real world.' Does it - the conception itself - exist without you?"

"I'm not talking about the conception."[6]

"What, then?"

I rubbed my face. "You expect me to believe nothing whatsoever exists independently of me?" My fingers had a strange smell to them, a mixture of resin and alcohol.

"I expect you to believe what you know to be true; no more, no less." She raised her eyebrows. "Follow your own

Rules for the Direction of the Mind. Or was that another one of your philosophical points?"

"Would Philosophy destroy the concept of a real, mind-independent, objective world?"

"You mean an 'objective, subjectless world'?" She laughed. "An easy victory."

"How can you say that?"

"Because no such world exists, René. You're thinking of an 'objective space,' an outside without an inside. The author of analytic geometry should know better! There can be no outside without an inside, no objects in space without a subject in time to which they appear. You desire a contradiction. You want to experience a conscious state that cannot possibly be experienced, to be the subject of a subjectless world."

"Is the sum of all worlds, then, reality?"

"No."

"Why?"

"No such sum is possible."

"Why not?"

"Because your concept, 'reality,' involves an 'objective world,' a 'super-world,' a consortium of worlds conceived in terms of a purely 'objective,' subjectless, totality of objects *and* subjects! You cannot help but think *objective world* even though buried in your understanding is the hidden meaning that a world, as such, necessarily requires both subject and object. No 'objective world' as conceived by you exists because no such world could possibly exist."

"Then who - what – are we? Tell me what we are."

"Here." Philosophy offered me her hand. "The dreams

that stuff is made of."

I took her hand. Her warm, delicate fingers, soft and inviting to the touch, smelled of lilac. I brought her hand within reach of my lips and for some reason bowed to it without a kiss, as one does with a married woman.

I caught myself in her eyes, awestruck suddenly by a numinous sense of the presence of the other - a being within me greater than myself. Telling myself this could not be possible, that she existed only in my head, I tried to imagine my sleeping body lying on its back with eyes closed. *Wake up,* I said to myself, *you're not here but there.* Projecting myself into that imagined bundle of conceived flesh, trying to resurrect myself into the 'real' world, I realized no, I was not 'there' but *here.* The word *there,* as I had just used it while thinking of a translucent image of a sleeping body referred ostensively not to a body made of flesh and blood but to a vaguely conceived image. My 'real' body was, I believed, asleep and lying down, a material substance made of flesh and blood, not this standing body made out of imagination. The body *I* was *in* was not that (vaguely imagined) lying body but this (vividly imagined, perceived, felt) standing body: the body I was in was not the body I believed I was in, and the body I believed I was in was not my body!

Like the dreamed stars hanging above me in the dreamed sky, both the conceived (i.e., 'real') body I believed I was in and the seen (i.e., 'experienced') body I believed was but an imaginary body in a dream were themselves imaginary, for both were dependent for their existence upon the subject, me. The body I seemed to be in was *here* and *imaginary* and the

13

body I thought I was in was *imaginary* and *nowhere.*[7] This was not methodological doubt but fear for my existence, an abyss of unknowing, a maelstrom of anxiety. *I am not doubting whether I have a real body, I am realizing I have no real body.* Something within me had begun to unravel. Or, should I say, to sew itself together? *I am the ghost in the theoretical machine; reality is my theory and my corpse.*

Philosophy flew back up onto her former perch. The moon had set, leaving a sky full of effervescent stars. Mt. Parnassus loomed above the ruins, grim, ominous, silent in the starlight pouring over each crevice like magnetic fluid, swimming in electric effluvia.

This all is in my head, I said to myself, still trying to wake up, *this all is in my head,* and I went on repeating my hollow incantation to reality: *this all is in my head . . .*

"Clasp your hands on top of your head," she said.

Startled, I looked up. "What am I, surrendering?"

"No; the defiant one."

I put my hands on top of my head.

"Is that your head?"

"Yes." A chill shook me.

"There," she said, pointing at my head, "is that where this dream exists? Inside there?"

"Yes," I said, knowing it was false.[8]

"Everything here - the sky, the ruins, this world entire - is contained within that head which you presently hold in those hands?"

"Yes." *No,* I thought, but could not say it.

"So these objects - the wall of this antechamber, the

14

temple, the stars – they all are contained–" she pointed again at me, "there, inside that head atop your shoulders?"

"Yes." *No.*

"Don't you see what I am asking?"

"No!" *Yes, yes,* I thought, but still I could not say it, not even to myself, not even in a dream, not even as the revelation divined existential shivers through my nonexistent spine. But I knew what she meant.

This was a dream. In this dream, a woman sat atop a wall, talking to a man. She had a body and head with eyes fixed upon the man. The man stood at the base of the wall, looking up at her. This man could think, feel, reason and wonder about himself and the world he was in. Perhaps the woman could too but the man believed she couldn't because he believed this was a dream, that she was a figment of his imagination, an object in his head. Except this man had no head. He had feet, legs, a torso, fingers, hands, arms and shoulders atop of which was not the head *she* was in but the world in which they both were in.

I was that man. I was the man in the dream who mistook his world for a head.

There is no light inside the head. Yet the 'scene before my eyes' presented itself to me as if the light I saw had traced the following geometrical path: from some light source (what – where – is the 'light' source in a dream?) to the 'surface' of the objects (as if they had an inside!) which in turn sent this 'reflected light' through space (what is the space, the medium of light, I see in a dream?) to my 'eyes' (what 'eyes' do I see with in a dream?) which in turn sent an impulse to my 'brain,'

15

causing these perceptions to exist as ideas in my 'mind.' This false geometry of dreams lay at the root of the illusion that the world in my experience was external to my mind, a mathematical self-deception written into the meaning of the 'scene before my eyes,' structuring my experience into a 'physical world.' For in fact no such geometrical path was involved in the generation of the objects in the dream. The 'eyes' through which I saw the dream were not eyes. The 'head' inside which I was situated was not a head but a world inside which there was no brain, no processor of information distinct from the mental objects of my perception. The nonexistent head I was in was but a vantage point from which I experienced the dream. The objects I saw 'outside' myself, including the headless body with the world atop its shoulders and the subject (myself) whom I took to be not a subject but my head, were generated not one from another (from the object to the subject via perception) but in one simultaneous act of consciousness.

"Point," ordered Philosophy, "point to where the head is within which this dream exists."

And point I did: at the wall, at the stars, at Mt. Parnassus, at the ground and at the ruins all around. The head I was in was everywhere and all around, for this was a dream and I was in it, yet nowhere, for what I was pointing at was not a head but a world. I asked myself: if this space surrounding me exists inside my head, where in relation to me, the dream subject, is the 'real' head inside which this dream and I exist - in what space? Where in relation to me is 'reality,' that glorious and infinitely empty womb inside which the real world exists? In what direction from me, within the subjective space inside which I exist as a conscious subject, is the objective space I conceive to be the container of me and of my world, the universe entire?

Pointing now the other way (thinking this cannot be my finger, I am asleep, my hands are at my sides), right between my eyes (thinking these are not my eyes, my eyes are closed), at myself (thinking this is not me but a representation of myself inside myself) staring at my finger (with what, I asked myself, with what?), I couldn't speak, I couldn't think. Reason had abandoned me to the circular ruins inside myself, trapped me in the logic of the impenetrable contradiction that existence is, one with everything, full of nothing, empty as a tautology. Inside the labyrinth at the center of the world I found myself without a face and I stood there pointing at the beast, unmasked, headless.[9]

What was I pointing at? Who was I pointing at? Who was pointing? Who?

"But I am not nothing," I cried. "I am not no one! *Who am I?*"

Suddenly the question wounded, it opened everything.

ENDNOTES

[1] *Meditations on the First Philosophy, in Which the Existence of God, and the Real Distinction of Mind and Body, Are Demonstrated,* by René Descartes, John Veitch trans., Open Court 1901, reprinted in Daniel Kolak, *The Mayfield Anthology of Western Philosophy,* Mayfield 1998.

[2] Her words, after all, were my words, my thoughts – they had to be, they were coming at me from somewhere within. This was a dream and she was a dream character. I did not believe in demons nor in possession. She was not a foreign soul but merely an aspect of myself, perhaps some part of me I had long ago in sculpting my philosophy hidden from myself. There is always that remaining part of your soul, unconvinced by your philosophy, that you have to exorcise from yourself to have a view; the philosophical dialectic: we make up our minds by halving them. Whole, we cannot remain on one side of an issue long enough to forget the view from the other side is just as flimsy and as good (everything works, when you are in it, *literally like a dream,* this is the secret wisdom of all religions). We thus divide and conquer ourselves: we become someone with a view and make that view our own. In this way your view becomes part of your identity. I had for a long time suspected this and perhaps that's who and what she was incarnate: my alter ego and philosophical antithesis rendered in the dramatic form of scholastic mythology and magic, a being within myself that I had banished from consciousness to become Descartes: Anti-Cartesius, now come back in the guise of the Goddess of Philosophy to haunt me, perhaps even to stake claim to my waking soul. The thought makes me laugh and shiver.

[3] I knew what she meant. Mersenne and I had often quarreled about it. Did the objects of mathematics refer to the world as it existed in itself, or were they themselves but descriptions, renderings of mental experiences? The scientifically inclined natural philosophers in our Paris circle insisted that the language of mathematics, unlike the terms of ordinary language, has a grip on reality (of course I no longer know what *that* means) - that mathematics can render the

world entire. (And of course by 'world' we in the Paris circle did not mean what Philosophy meant.) I myself was drawn to this view and had in my youth hoped to transfer some of its methodological insights into the new philosophy. The more skeptical philosophers among us, on the other hand, viewed mathematics the same way the Pyrhonnian skeptics once viewed ordinary language and experience, as being a representation of purely mental constructions: mathematics viewed in this way is merely the set of tautologies, logical but therefore empty. Mathematics viewed in this way is but a symbolic container, as experience is, but only an idealized rendition of what is already in the mind to begin with such that, on this view, mathematics is as impotent as natural language is to render 'reality.'

[4] I marveled at the spontaneous subtlety and swiftness of her delivery. She implied that the sort of space and time she meant were not to be understood in some purely mathematical, or formal, sense. She did not mean by "space" the specification of such and such coordinates, that is, space understood in geometrical terms, or time understood as a numerical sequence or series, that is, time conceived in arithmetical terms. Rather, she was talking about the space one experiences and likewise for time - not in terms of a physical theory but as psychological time actually experienced. (In other words, time and space in the dream existed for me and may or may not have calibrated with any aspect of formal space and time as conceived in mathematical and physical theory as existing independently of me.) She thus meant phenomenal, subjective space, and phenomenal, subjective time (and experienced, not merely described, as such). By thus involving the subject in *her* description, she managed cleverly to fix the reference of "world" to a essentially subjective rendering of what, ordinarily, I would have wanted to call 'reality.' She was, indeed, very clever (and this of course pleased me, since I considered her 'my own,' albeit unconscious, creation) at setting up the verbal pieces of her conceptual argument in advance. I do not know which one of us wrote this note.

[5] Once again I thought how strange it was to be having this argument with myself in a dream. What I had meant was that dreams are stories we tell ourselves with the help of mental pictures. But she had retorted with the crucial difference: dreams are not just pictures any more than waking experience consists of just pictures; there is in both cases a point of view involved, and not merely in the way, say, a scene in a painting is rendered from a certain perspective. In a dream, as in waking experience, the point of view is not something expressed as a perspectival arrangement of objects in the scene but is, itself, a projection of *you*, the viewer, into the scene such that it becomes *your* experience and – this is crucial - from the 'inside.' That is why she was bringing in, rightly, the notion of the subject. Whether in a dream or in a waking state, the subject is the apparent location within the scene of the experiencing entity one takes oneself to be.

[6] She had cut off my escape route and I knew it. In waking life I might have tried to counter and the discussion would at this point no doubt have ceased being philosophical and turned merely rhetorical. But this was a dream and I knew therefore that I was only arguing with myself; what would be the point of winning? Yet I was afraid of losing.

[7] In other words, can you refer to your body in a dream? In one sense, of course you can; you can say "my body is at home, in bed, asleep." The problem with this is that as you are saying it you find yourself not at home in bed and unconscious but, as in the present case, standing somewhere. Now, you can try to say, as in the present case, "this body is not my body," but now you're shredding logic's gears, stripping both the sense (*Sinn*) and reference, or meaning (*Bedeutung*) from your expressions as such. (See my *Wittgenstein's Tractatus*, Mayfield 1998, and Gottlob Frege's *Veber Sinn und Bedeutung*, 1892, trans. Daniel Kolak in *The Mayfield Anthology of Western Philosophy*, Mayfield 1998). cit.) Of course you can wave your hands, proverbial or otherwise, and try to indicate yourself out of the philosophical black hole but in so doing you throw out the whole of your actual being there (*Dasein;* see my discussion of Heidegger in

20

From the Presocratics to the Present: A Personal Odyssey,
Mayfield 1998, pp. 256-260) into an abyss of insubstantiality.

[8] This was strange. Language said that this, what 'I'
'held' in 'my' hands, was 'my' head. But the truth of the
matter was otherwise. "My head is not my head" was a true
statement; once you see the sense in which this is not a
contradiction you will have successfully severed the semantics
of experience from the syntax of theory (but only for a while –
you have to move quickly and then to keep moving). For how
did I know this, except by means of language? Philosophy
thus neither uses nor destroys language but turns language
against itself. And that is the sense in which I would say it was
literally true that I had finally lost my head.

[9] The point I had just made to myself in the dream of
course holds equally in dream and waking states. For instance:
right now it seems to you that you are where your face is, on
the surface of your skin, perched just in front of your face,
looking outside at the world, as if your insides were behind
you. But your insides are in front of you and all around! We
exist backwards, upside down, inside out.

TWO

THE
MASK
OF
CONSCIOUSNESS

Just as comedians are counseled not to let shame appear on their foreheads, and so put on a mask: so likewise, now that I am to mount the stage of the world, where I have so far been spectator, I come forward in a mask.

René Descartes

"WHO DO YOU THINK YOU ARE?"
"René Descartes?"[1]
Philosophy leaned forward and peered down at me from the wall, her elbows on her knees, her face in her hands.

22

"Why Descartes?" She tapped her sandaled heels playfully against the stone. A pair of chameleons escaped from a crack and scurried across the wall to hide into separate holes.

"It's who I . . . how I remember myself."

"Is that who you are?"

"Why else would I remember?"

"In order to forget."

From within me a barrage of memory loomed forth in self defense: at the age of sixteen arriving at La Flèche, with my father explaining to the Dean how I liked to stay in bed until noon and I had felt so embarrassed; taking Pierre Chanut's bad advice and going to Sweden; as a young man joining Prince Maurice's Nassau army; getting drunk in a pub in Breda with Isaac Beeckman, arguing with him at Dortmund about the mathematics of Ramon Llull; the cabin in Neuberg between the Bavarian campaigns, settling down to write near the logs inside that fiery winter womb etched in chiaroscuro; the mystical dream on St. Martin's Eve; Marin Mersenne, Claude Mydorge, Étienne de Villebressieu, Jean de Silhon, a melange of half-forgotten names and faces communing in that eternal City of Philosophy whose streets wind through Paris and stretch into the shadows of infinity; Gisbert Voet whom I should have run through with a blade; Monsieur N., the stranger in my recurring dream; my two Francines; making love with Princess Elizabeth; an open grave in the churchyard at Ste. Geneviève du Mont . . .

"What do you remember?" Philosophy's gentle voice returned me to the dream.

"Everything and nothing. Myself, yesterday. Last night.

Last month's carriage ride. My argument with the Queen. Sweden is so cold." Thinking about my argument with Christina I recalled my earlier dream in which I had come to Delphi in search of myself and it made me realize what all the remembering had made me forget: *you are not in Delphi.*

"Is that you?"

"In the memory? As far as I can tell." I looked for a knit of identity among the collage of broken images, an assemblage of stained glass, luminous pieces of a dream. "My arrival at La Flèche, for instance, with my overbearing and overprotective father - you must understand, my mother died shortly after I was born, and he . . . why am I telling you this! Anyway, in those past states of consciousness I see myself, in the Dean's office at La Flèche, with my father, I'm standing next to my father . . ."

"Inside the memory itself? You're there, seeing your surrounding objects?"

"When you put it that way, no, of course, I am not there but here, remembering."

"Where is 'here'?"

"Inside my . . . in this dream. In the present."

"You see yourself? In the present - dreaming or awake, do you see the subject?"

"No. I don't see the subject. I am the subject. I see images, I don't make them up, they make me up. Just as these surrounding ruins tell me where I am with such authority, so convincingly, that no amount of reasoning can dissolve me out of this space, so from within me memories tell me who I am."

"Be careful: is this wall an image? Am I an image?"

"Yes . . . *no!*" I saw my error. "No. I believe in theory that's what you are because I believe this is a dream. But that's not what I see. I see . . . objects."

"Good. Now look at your memory. Does memory consist of subject and objects?"

Again I looked. What did I see? Dim, translucent images. And suddenly I realized what she wanted me to see.

"Memories appear not as objects but as what they are: images, mental phenomena. Whereas you and the wall . . . my God, but I was on the verge of realizing this moments ago, only . . . I couldn't quite see it. Memories appear as images because the subject is missing. My God." I stared up at her. "Is that what makes dreams seem less real than waking states? Because remembering a dream one is looking not at objects but memories – images? And why inside a dream waking states appear fuzzy, unreal and tenuous, exactly the way that in my waking states dreams appear to be?"

She nodded. "Now you see it."

It was true, I could see that it was true. Remembering what I take to be my waking states I correctly ascribe the property of memory not to the states remembered but to myself in the act of remembering: I say, 'I am fuzzy on that,' 'I don't remember it in order,' and so on. Whereas remembering what I take to be dream states I falsely ascribe these same properties of memory – discontinuity, lack of clarity, and so on – not to myself in the act of remembering but to the remembered states themselves: I say, 'The dream was fuzzy,' 'Scenes switched haphazardly,' 'there was no continuity to the events,' and so on. In neither case do such judgments have anything to do with the quality of my states of consciousness. In both cases they render the nature and quality of memory, not experience.

Looking up beyond Mt. Parnassus into the starry heavens of my imagination, wondering with what ink the mind drew its objects and on what canvas, I realized suddenly the connection between my favorite haunt in Paris - Monparnasse - and this ancient place in Greece from which that name derives. How strange, I thought, that Delphi and Paris were connected by a white temple on a hill, cheered on by a thought, a name, a dream.

"And you see now the role of memory? Does memory reveal the nature of your identity, or hide you from yourself?"

"Memory binds me together over time," I said. "It connects me from one moment to the next. Memory gives to my individual states of consciousness a sense of continuity."

"In time, yes. The feeling you are that self here and now and nowhere no one else, no other. In this way memory disconnects you from the rest of your world in the present, it becomes a wall between self and other. In space, this space you are in: what creates the illusion you are there, an embodied self surrounded by ruins, in the presence of another? Why don't you see this whole dream for what it is, one amorphous being? Because memory in the space of your experience divorces you from yourself by 'connecting' you to an image of yourself as extended in time, it divides you from all the rest of your world."

Her words were shattering. I understood what this voice within me said instantly and without argument, truth divined in

26

its moment of expression. The meaning of the fundamental sentence of my existence – 'I think, therefore I am,' - had increased a million fold – and by what? – through loss of self-reference. The revelation that in the space of my experience it was none other than identification with self that individuated me from all the rest of my world at a time, left me hanging in the moment, suspended inside myself.

"But where would I be without memory, what would I be, who?" I had suddenly such a strong and wild sense of my own presence, like slipping on ice toward a precipice, out of control you catch yourself off guard: unexpected and exhilarating, provided you're not dead, if the fall doesn't kill you. "I could wake up from a dream and be someone else entirely, completely different memories, think nothing of it."

I tried to imagine what that would be like. I could not dissociate from my identification as Descartes to an abstract image of being 'someone other than myself, I know not who,' so I tried instead to make myself believe I was Mersenne.[2] Here I am, I said to myself, in this existential nightmare, not Descartes but Mersenne dreaming I am Descartes. Let me suppose, then, that I have lost my true Mersennian memories and all my Cartesian memories are false. In that case I, the present subject in the dream (mis)identified by false memories as Descartes, am and will be correctly identified upon waking by true memories as Mersenne. I could imagine it but not believe it: the intellectual recognition of the possibility that I was someone else did not produce in me the slightest doubt regarding my identity, nor did it dispel in the least my feeling of certainty that I was Descartes.

This bothered me. First of all, why should I be able to imagine being someone else other than Descartes, when clearly I could in no way imagine *Descartes* being someone other than Descartes? In that sense – albeit a purely formal, logical sense – the mere possibility of being someone else liberated *me,* the subject, from my *self.*[3] *I am not who I am.*

"I can't imagine what that would be like," I said, "to be anyone other than Descartes. But I think I would be much surprised to find myself believing, with this same feeling of certainty, that I was anyone else–"

"Surprised by what?"

"Finding out I was . . . someone else."

"Who would be surprised? If you woke up to find you were 'someone else' other than Descartes, would it be Descartes who was 'someone else?'"

"Of course not, no. It would be me, the subject, in this dream identified as Descartes, who upon waking would find himself identified as . . . whoever."

"And who would that be?"

"A different self, I don't know!"

"Wouldn't it be *you?*"

"Not Descartes. Another self."

"Yet *you.*"

"But I wouldn't remember anything."

"Is not identity preserved in either case? Amnesia is not the same as death. Even if you 'woke up' as someone else, with completely different memories, an entirely different self in another world, with no recollection of your previous life, would identity not be preserved?"

"By what? There's no connection!"

"Yet you would survive," she said.

"Descartes wouldn't."

"What about *you?*"

"Me, *who?*"

"The subject."

"Without a self? Are you saying I could be anyone?"

"Could be? Or *are?* Look, suppose you woke up as Mersenne. Would you *then* be surprised to be a different self, other than Descartes?"

"You mean, would I be surprised to be a different self – which I would then assume was and always had been my one and only 'true self' – viewing through a different mask another world which I would then assume was and always had been my one and only reality? No! What I would then be surprised by – perhaps even rightly disturbed – would be the recollection of having ever believed I was Descartes. As Mersenne I would find it as impossible to doubt my identity as I now find it impossible to doubt – except in a purely intellectual, theoretical sense – that I am Descartes. Indeed, the sensation of doubting my identity, like the sensation of identity itself – like all my beliefs, whether in dream or waking states – are not under my conscious control! Unlike the *I am* - the conscious sensation of existing - the sensation of identity – *I am someone* - and the sensation of non-identity – *I am no one else* – prove nothing! I am and know that I am in a way I cannot ever know or perhaps even *be* who I am. For in no way can I doubt *that* I am, where as I can doubt, at least intellectually, *who* I am."

"There you have it," she said. "The world is your dream

but the self is your dream too and you are the subject in the middle, the fulcrum of consciousness."

I felt dizzy and disoriented. I could feel myself trying to wake up, wanting desperately to forget the dream and remember myself into a different reality and yet, at the same time, dreading it. I tried to picture, to imagine, my 'true identity." All I achieved was the inner identification of myself as a self extended in time. And when I tried to dissociate from any such self-image, what then? The image of no image is itself an image: a blank, an emptiness, an infinite space with absolutely nothing in it, a space of infinite possibility. Not nothing, no, I am almost but not quite nothing. I am the hollow nothing.

Once again memory pulled me out of the abyss. I remembered the plight of my friend Gaspard Teyssier, an actor who knew his roles better than he knew himself, who could give up one role only to take up another. He could never be without a mask, always he had his role to play, whether in the theater or upon the stage of the world. Between roles Gaspard played at being himself, his greatest role, to hide the darkness of his talent, the hidden flaw that made him a great actor, the greatest of our time: that behind his many masks he was no one. That is what we said of him, amongst ourselves, never to his face – a face that off stage betrayed a frail vulnerability, too beautiful and feminine to belong to any man, as if he were a composite of all humankind, a blank expression of the form of infinite possibility. We admired him in our Paris circle and made a secure place for him because he was to any one of us a perfect mirror. He, in turn, befriended us because we knew what his audience could not imagine: the ineffaceable horror that made it possible for him to be anyone was the knowledge that he was no one, the emptiness of his existence, vanity, pure, existential, vanity, not absolute nothingness, that would have been a relief. Behind his face was the nothingness of the mirror.

How odd, I thought, to feel suddenly less like myself than someone who was so like no one that he could be virtually anyone. I saw clearly and distinctly that if I who am now Descartes could wake up as Mersenne (or Teyssier – this would have been the perfect dream for him) the explanation would have to be either that it was I, the subject, who was first identified as Descartes and then Mersenne, or that identified as Mersenne I was now a completely new and different subject from the one formerly identified as Descartes. But what then could possibly distinguish the subject, qua subject, here in the dream identified as Descartes, from the subject identified there upon waking as Mersenne? How does one demarcate boundaries between subjects, distinguish one subject from another? The content of experience by which I at that present moment was distinguished from my imagined future self was not a difference of life and death between one being and another, but only of identification with memory, a boundary within one numerically identical being who is many selves: Descartes now and Mersenne (or Teyssier) then, even though Descartes and Mersenne and Teyssier are not one self but three. But what then am I even looking for when I inquire into my personal identity as a being whose consciousness is in this way always bordered yet never bound, as Descartes in one dream yet possibly in another as someone else?

I began thus to understand what I could in no way bring myself to believe. Remembering myself dismembers me, it divides the mind into self and other, subject and object, thereby divorcing me from the rest of my world. Seeing myself 'there' in the 'past' obscures me from myself in the present, it keeps me from seeing myself whole. Identification as a self alienates me from my world, it fragments my existence. At each moment identification dissociates subject from object, thereby creating a world within and into which I am projected and bound through identification as, in that moment, René Descartes, a memory-bound, 'objectified subject:' the *illusion* of identity over time achieved through the illusion of non-identity with objects at a time! The subject is thus dissociated - projected, as it were - from the actuality of the present moment into time, spread out backwards and forwards until it is aware of itself only as the self, a mind within the mind, divorced from its objects in space through self-identification in time. That is how association of states of consciousness over time with each other – the self, René Descartes - dissociates me as the subject in any present moment of my existence from all the rest of my world, strengthening thereby through sense of self the illusion that the world of my experience is not my own, a dream, as the self is, but an external thing, 'reality.' The feeling of my own existence as a self is achieved through the feeling of my nonexistence as the surrounding objects in the space of my experience. This truth, obscured through identification as a self revealed the world of my experience to

32

be external only to the self, not to the subject.[4]

"I think I am finally beginning to understand," I said, pressing my hands against the wall. "The distance between you and me, between me and this wall, is no distance at all. This is not a geometrical space of objective points with separate identities that we are in but an identification space of subjective points. This world consists not partly of external relations but entirely of internal relations. Identification says otherwise but identification is not the reflexive self-relation that identity is, between the subject and itself - *I* am *I* - but a one-way associative relation between the subject and its self-image – *I* am *you*."

Nodding, she sighed, slowly, wistfully. "You and I are not two beings but two aspects of one and the same being, that's right." She opened her arms, letting the folds of her robe blow in the cool, soft breeze. "These are the self-imposed boundaries without which experience would be impossible and selves as such could not exist. I seem to exist outside you; what looks like a boundary between self and other is but a border drawn within your mind, achieved through identification as a self inside your own world. In this way the subject comes to see itself identified not as subject but as an external object – for instance, me."

"If that's so," I said, "and I know it must be because this is a dream – why can't I control you at will? Why does everything not respond directly to my wishes and desires? This wall, for instance." I slapped the wall. "It is not made of stone. It is an idea, a construction in my mind, a fabrication. Did *I* fabricate it? I'm not *consciously* doing it. Can I go through it? Can I make it disappear? No! In that sense it clearly and distinctly exists independently of me, independently of any conscious action on my part. Yet I know because this is a dream that this wall does not exist independently of me! It is a *mental* wall. *Why* then can I not go through it? I know it must be my own mind that causes this wall to exist along with all its apparent properties, up to and including impenetrability. How does the mind become impenetrable to itself, when this very boundary is not a border between one being and another, and I am that being? Will you answer me this, Philosophy?"

She gave me a quick, delightful smile with a slight lift of her fine eyebrows. "Is this not the same situation as in your waking states?" She leaned forward from atop the wall like a beautiful gargoyle. "You assume what you control is you and what you do not control is not you. That is how you achieve the illusion of an external, mind-independent world, the illusion of reality. It haunts you does it not? Even in your dreams!" Her lips cracked into a grin. "An illusion so perfect that revealing it makes no difference. A deception so devious that even once you know it you are powerless to stop it, even when you know it's you, still you can do nothing about it but stand in awe and be amazed at how you have trapped yourself into existence, how you have made out of yourself your own victim."

"This is absurd." I pressed against the wall, feeling its resistance. I ran my hands across its warm, rough surface. Out of frustration I slapped the wall again, harder; I felt pain. How ridiculous, I thought, to be able to think truly and correctly the

34

thought, 'This wall exists only in my mind, I am making this up,' while realizing, at the same time, that I was unaware as to *how* I was doing it! Neither Delphi - my objects - nor Descartes - my self - were transparent to me, their conscious subject! Everything in a dream exists through me yet somehow slips out of my control. Thus the frighteningly clear and distinct sense in which both the objects situating me in Delphi and the images identifying me as Descartes seemed 'real' was this: in neither case was I consciously making them up. I, the conscious subject, who because this was a dream was one with everything in my world, was not directly in control of myself nor of the world that I was in. Yet I knew I had to be connected to these 'other' aspects of myself - aspects which I could in no way consciously control.

I put my hands back on the wall and pushed with all my strength - as if somehow, this time, I could trick myself into tricking myself. I couldn't, yet still I *believed* I could, in principle, because I knew the wall to be a mental object, an idea that existed only in virtue of being perceived. Something - someone? - was preventing any further penetration into the inner workings of myself. At the same time, this something or someone was pushing me on to continue - as if a tug of war existed within me - a war of wills? But how could that be? What against what - who against whom? If the subject is the one who perceives and thinks its world into existence, the *I am* and the *I think*, the will belongs with the subject; so it *had* to be *me*, yet it was not me!

Were it not for the fact that this was a dream, I would have believed - as no doubt you presently do in your 'waking' state - that what explained the rigidity of the wall in my experience was the rigidity of its underlying physical substance. But in dreams there is no underlying rigidity of physical substance that corresponds to the perceived rigidity of objects[5] - none whatsoever! - and yet in dreams objects can and do behave just as they do in waking experience. Thus the problem of the wall: what could possibly explain the fact that for all my will and effort *I* could not go through that wall? What in my dream or in *any* experience could possibly explain the wall's rigidity - except that ideas can themselves be *rigid*, behaving with a will all their own, as impenetrable to each other as stone is to stone? That a purely ideal object could behave exactly as a material object, was a fact. A dream - any dream in which one seemed to encounter rigid objects - is a clear and distinct expression of that fact. Indeed, the existence of dreams itself is a clear and distinct expression of the nature, structure, and resilience of ideas.

Of course I believed a stone could go through an imaginary wall, just as I believed a musket ball could at any moment during that dream have pierced my brain, thereby successfully ending this existential nightmare with a bullet. But just as a stone cannot so easily move through a stone so, likewise, an idea cannot so easily move through another idea. Had I been awake (meaning: philosophically asleep, unenlightened) I would no doubt have assumed without question that the wall was made of stone, that my hand was made of flesh, and that what explained the situation in my experience was that flesh does not go through stone.[6] But the wall upon which Philosophy sat in her regal pose as if upon a throne was *not* made of stone. The wall upon which she sat was an idea, a fabrication of the mind, such stuff as dreams are made of - or, as she had quipped, *such dreams as stuff is made of* - just as the hand pressing against the wall - my hand - was not made of flesh.

I held up my hand: *This is not my hand!* Of course. My hand, too, was not a hand but the representation of a hand. The hand I was holding up in the dream and looking at was an idea of a hand - an *objectified idea*. Staring at the idea of my hand I moved it slowly to the wall and pressing against the (objectified) idea of the wall I had an absolutely astounding thought, unbelievably bizarre in its minimalistic simplicity, an insight as profound as any I have ever had, up to and including the realization in the act of thinking of the indubitability of my existence: *the idea of a hand does not go through the idea of a wall.*

So then what about me, the subject identified as this perceiver, thinker, knower, this self? I am also identified as an idea, an *objectified idea*, which is what the self is. Here, then, was the simple principle that made *any* experience as such seem real, whether in a dream or waking state:[7] *ideas sustain their borders against other ideas.*

I began thinking about this new insight in a way I had rarely been able to think about anything in my waking experience, with a patience and lucidity of mind that made waking consciousness seem like a dim shadow of a dream. *The idea of a hand does not go through the idea of a wall.* The sentence kept repeating itself in me as if afraid of being too soon forgotten. I asked myself: could the concept of a wall outside my mind made of stone and the concept of a hand outside my mind made of flesh explain why my *present* hand – the hand with outstretched fingers that I was looking at (not the one I dimly imagined to be clenched beneath the covers, at 'my' side) – did not go through that wall? No! What could be clearer than that? Did I, the conscious subject, exist outside myself, beyond the mind, or inside? Inside, of course, always. Well, but what about my waking states? The same! After all, I am never located in some world outside myself, beyond the mind. How could I be? For me, the subject, to somehow project myself outside the world in which I am by necessity (if there is to be conscious experience) required to exist, would require nothing short of witchcraft. The experience of solidity could in no way be explained by the concept of the solidity of the material world! How *could* it be? If physical substance exists – let it be so - it would not and could not be found beneath the objects in my experience,[8] nor within them, but would have to exist altogether outside experience, beyond the subject. How could experience search inside itself for what is beyond experience – the subject move outside itself, into a world beyond the subject? Impossible! The wall in my dream upon which Philosophy sat mocking me with her phantasmagoric grin made this perfectly clear.

Suppose, I asked myself, that I took this dream wall apart, studied it, broke it down to its elements, to see what it was made of. This activity – dream science! - would be as futile as trying to tunnel my way out of a dream by digging through the floor! Would a microscope help me see through the phenomena to the underlying physical substance? Would a telescope help me, the subject identified as a self within the mind, see beyond my mind? The whole of science suddenly revealed itself to be an entirely laughable enterprise, pure sophistry. I, the dream philosopher could become a dream scientist and turn the temple of Delphi into a laboratory, build elaborate instruments . . . could I thereby study the properties of matter, of physical substance, of the brain itself? Absurd! All science, with its most sophisticated technological gadgetry, is but dream epistemology, an elaborate form of introspection. That's what in our waking states we fail to understand - that even our 'tests' and 'experiments' are themselves but constructions within a dream, that to the degree that they 'work' makes them no less deceptive, no less nefarious.

Clearly, objects in dreams have no underlying physical substance of which they are representations. A dream and everything in it is purely subjective, a mental construction. That for all my will and effort I could in that dream not go through that wall made the notion of physical walls superfluous to the question of why conscious experience is as it is; mental walls are sufficiently impenetrable to build an entire world, a world of pure consciousness. One had to see it but once and but for a moment to see and understand. There may be another world, a material world of physical substance - and I do have the concept of such a world - but the physical world concept in no way explains the actual world of conscious experience being the way it is.

Why, I wondered, had all this never occurred to me before? After all, was not thinking - the paradigm of mental activity - itself law-governed, as was the imagination with its own logical rules? Are not the tautologies of logic as rigid as they are empty? Does not modus ponens preserve and sustain itself in the mind, devouring other structures and building up others? Ordinarily, we conceive of physical matter to explain the resilience of our ideal representations; we regard ideas as insubstantial, mere images in relation to physical substance. But do not our own dreams reveal how ideas can themselves be as resilient in relation to each other – become objects – just as matter conceived in terms of physical substance can? We speak of the 'clash' of ideas, the 'stubbornness' of ideas – here inside the mind the subjective world consisted not of things but thoughts, ideas – was not this world of mind within the mind as impenetrable as any world conceived outside the mind? You will say no, to conceive of a purely spiritual world of ideas without substance as having a rigid structure is impossible. But, again: a dream is such a world. Furthermore, such a conception is *not* impossible. We can and do conceive of God.

Furthermore, and most importantly, what was true of my external identifications was equally true of my internal identifications. What was true of Delphi was true of Descartes, that is, true of me and of everything I knew as myself, including my thoughts, beliefs, opinions, theories, and – especially – my memories. Just as the impenetrable walls of my surrounding world identified me in the dream to be at Delphi and nowhere else, so the contours of my memories identified me in the dream to be Descartes and no one else. The walls of inner memory making up my Cartesian self and the walls of outward experience making up my Delphic world both were impenetrable to my consciousness, to the conscious subject identified as a self, Descartes, to *me*. The mind within the mind within which I subsisted identified as a self surrounded by all manner of objects, my world entire, was opaque to me. The embodied self and I, the subject of my world, am thus not merely locked inside the world from the outside, I am also from the inside locked outside myself as subject into this headless body, inside the world that I am in. *To be is to be trapped, outside yourself, inside the world, inside yourself.*

Yet all these wondrous insights made me even more perplexed and sullen. Something was missing, a critical aspect of my understanding. What could possibly explain all these facts being as they are, the nature of ideas behaving as if they had a mind of their own? These were, after all, not other identified *subjects* in my presence – this I firmly believed - but aspects of myself, the subject. What then held all the aspects of my world apart and related them together in this dynamic way? It all seemed to require *more* than me, yet I could not see how it could involve anything more than me, since everything there in that dream *was* me. So then, how?

I leaned against the wall and still as if to mock me against my will the wall supported me. The wall seemed in itself to be an effect of something other than me, other than myself. But what? Again (I had to keep reminding myself), matter here in the dream was out of the question. Again I pushed, full force. Still nothing. The mechanisms of my pushing and the mechanisms of the wall's resistance, like the mechanisms of thought, for all my effort were hidden out of my reach, beyond the subject identified as a self. But where, in relation

41

to me, were the forces that bound me to myself in this dream and how could I know them, reach them? Some other subject, another will? But how could that be, when this was a dream and I was everything in that dream, including myself? Yet there had to be some walled connection, some point of contact, between the mechanisms structuring the dream and making it possible for me to exist as a subject identified from without by all manner of objects, identified from within by all manner of images. So how could I find the mechanisms of this, my own mind, when there was nowhere *else* to look? It seemed pointless for me, as Descartes in a dream, to try to look for someone or something else besides myself within myself, to try to break through the impenetrable feeling that I am not just someone, anyone, but that I am this someone, this particular subject having this dream. The subject is, by definition and by experience, a unity. So it could not be some other subject, unless it was myself, and I could not see how it could possibly be myself, since I was not *aware* of existing in any sort of opposition against myself.

Still I did not give up (as if I could). I tried as my next move (against whom? Myself?) to retrace my thoughts to see if I had missed a path out of this tortuous dream labyrinth. Here before me stood a dream wall, an ideal object, a mental construction more stubborn than any physical substance could ever be. Could I chisel this wall, if it did not want to be chiseled? How? Any chisel I could possibly bring to it would be but a mental chisel, as would the hand holding the chisel be but a dream hand, as would be the dream man pounding with all his might upon the dream wall. Furthermore, here 'inside' me, the subject identified as Descartes, my self, was the image of myself as a continuously existing, spatially extended entity remembered over time: I had memories, along with the peculiar feeling of being who I seemed to be at that moment and no one else, I had a name, a past, a personality, a set of beliefs, a way I talked to myself and to others, and so on. Could I change at will what I believed about myself, thought to be true? How? I could say to myself, "I am Socrates," "I am not French," "I am Greek," "I am not dreaming that I am at Delphi, I am in Stockholm," and so on, but these words in no way affected the course of my external or internal identifications; such thoughts could not and did not change the experience of finding myself at Delphi, Descartes among the ruins. Yet I still believed with all my confidence that if only my 'real eyes' would open Delphi would vanish and Stockholm would reappear. But I had neither power to resist nor to question these feelings in any meaningful and non-verbal sense, any more than I could alter the images out of which were constructed my memories or the objects comprising the ruins of Delphi.

What I saw now even more clearly than before bothered me still more: the entire contents of my consciousness flowed into my consciousness from beyond my consciousness! Whether from 'above' or from 'below' – whether the nature of the world containing me was intelligent or a blind machine – I had no way of knowing. The awareness that this was so and that I existed caught in the act of being aware of my existence – self-consciousness, which is what I was and am – made me utterly powerless to affect the contents of consciousness. So I wondered: from where flows the content of my awareness of myself, of my world, of my ideas and my thoughts, of my experience entire? How does the mind inside the mind, identified subject and individuated object, divided within and from itself through identification as self, exclusively conjoin itself to one part of its world in an act of self-consciousness? How are the contents of consciousness constructed, gathered, organized – by what? It all seemed so utterly impossible: the objectified ideas identifying me at Delphi and the subjectified ideas identifying me as Descartes were my own ideas and yet I, the conscious subject, was bound against myself as if by force of the simultaneous presence of 'another,' God-like subject, nowhere present. I was bound by my own ideas, ideas that think, ideas with memories, ideas that in my own case believe they are a man, this man, René Descartes. It made me shiver. Were ideas themselves not merely logical machines, blind forces in which I lived and was bound to exist in through my identifications, but, themselves living spirits, subjects like myself? Were ideas the corporeal vessels of being? Were ideas not just mechanical but alive? But then to whom, to what, do *we* belong? What is the nature of the connection between ideas in which I live and me, this I, the knowing unknown presence within the idea, the insubstantial illumination of existence within the conceptual machine, the subject of the world? Was consciousness itself a being beyond any categories of thought? All my life I had conceived the mind-body problem in terms of the nature of the connection and interaction between material and immaterial substances. Now I saw the even more perplexing puzzle, an impossible conundrum: the mind-mind problem.[9]

I stared at Philosophy still sitting silently atop the wall, inscrutable, eminently beautiful against the star-filled night sky. She remained stoic, impenetrable, staring, waiting – for what? Judging?

"Why do you not help me? Why do you keep me prisoner like this, inside my own dream? *Who are you?*"

She picked up the scepter but not the books and laid it gently across her lap. "Am I not by your own words the goddess who consoled Boethius?"

"That's just it. Between his now defunct consciousness and my own you did not exist. You are but an imaginative idea, a fanciful apparition, a dream object animated by the light of my own consciousness. You do not persist over time, you have no identity beyond the mind that conceives and perceives you."

"Am I not the *same* goddess who consoled Boethius?"

"There is no such entity."

She feigned anger. "Awaiting death the man lay in chains, shunned and ridiculed, tortured . . . know you any who could produce as beautiful a poem as did he who launched me across the darkness of the ages into the light of your own soul?"

"In fiction, Philosophy consoled Boethius; in reality, Boethius consoled Boethius. It is his text that brought you to me, words without a soul."

"I grant you the identity but deny the distinction."

"But you're a work of fiction. You're not conscious."

She raised her eyebrows seductively. "Prove it."

"That you do not exist?" It made me laugh. "Easy. I - or, at least, the person having this dream, whatever be his true identity - am not the possible but the *actual* subject to whom those waking states, remembered as 'Descartes arriving at La Flèche' - no, as 'I arriving at La Flèche . . . no, wait . . . oh! I see . . . perhaps not. No, no, no - definitely they are not the same! I just again saw . . . my God, the self is not the dreamer but the dream, I am not who I am, that's the proof–"

"You are on the right track . . ." suddenly, she stopped. "Except here you must be more careful than before. We come around the same bend, only higher." She paused. "Who then is the dreamer?"

"I have no choice but to assume it is Descartes, a man presently asleep on his deathbed."

"Are we characters in Descartes' dream?"

"Except I'm the subject and you're an object! Or, at the very least, I am a subject that appears as a subject, where as you are a subject that appears as an object."

She smiled. "How do you know this?"

"How do I know I exist? Is that what you are asking?" I laughed. "We're back to *that?*"

"For the moment, yes. Same bend, only higher." She paused. "Well?"

"Because I cannot doubt that I exist."

"Neither can a nonexistent being."

"Very funny."

"It's true, isn't it?"

"But even if I am presently deceived about everything else - as in a sense, since I am dreaming, I am deceived - such that I doubt whether the year is 1650 and I am René Descartes dreaming a most extraordinary dream, the fact that I doubt this itself verifies that something - the act of doubting, at the very least - is going on. Be it a confused and deluded or a lucid and brilliant, this state is and I am that."

"Is that your proof?"

"The proof of *I am* is already contained in the *I think*. To think is to exist. I have already by thinking proved it to myself to be so. Even if I am at all moments deceived about everything else - if there is no Earth as such, no physical universe, no matter - as would be the case were some malicious demon or God deceiving me about everything, the conscious state of being deceived is not a nothing but a something, there is therefore something and I am it."

"How do you know this? Wait - I'm asking."

"I feel my own presence here in this dream–"

"Words," she said. "Mere words."

"Words? Not words, no. Thoughts."

"What is the difference?"

"You can put words on a page," I said. "Words are not thoughts. They are, at best, symbolic representations of thoughts, as numerals are symbolic representations of numbers. Words have no insideness, there is no one there inside those inkblots, no subject. Words express, or symbolize, or represent the author's thoughts. Words–"

"And you are not that?" She raised her eyebrows.

"I am not words, nor anything like words! No. I am not a book. I am not made of inkblots and pulp. I am conscious. I am not a bundle of symbols! This is not a book."

47

"How do you know?"

"The feeling of my own existence–"

"Can you prove you actually have this? Aside from your verbal rendering."

"There is . . . nothing to prove. It is being proved as it is happening, to me, by me, in the very occurrence of these conscious states."

"What is being proved?"

"That these conscious states exist as such. I cannot doubt the presence of my own consciousness as it appears to me."

Philosophy opened up one of her books, a small octavo volume with gold leaf, and read to me a passage I recognized instantly, for I had written it; it was from my own book:

> "I noticed that whilst I thus wished to think all things false, it was absolutely essential that the 'I' who thought this should be somewhat, and remarking that this truth 'I think, therefore I am' was so certain and so assured that all the most extravagant suppositions brought forward by the skeptics were incapable of shaking it, I came to the conclusion that I could receive it without scruple as the first principle of the Philosophy for which I was seeking.
>
> And then, examining attentively that which I was, I saw that I could conceive that I had no body, and that there was no world nor place where I might be; but yet that I could not for all that conceive that I was not. On the contrary, I saw from the very fact that I thought of doubting the

truth of other things, it very evidently and certainly followed that I was; on the other hand if I had only ceased from thinking, even if all the rest of what I had ever imagined had really existed, I should have no reason for thinking that I had existed. From that I knew that I was a substance the whole essence or nature of which is to think, and that for its existence there is no need of any place, nor does it depend on any material thing; so that this 'me,' that is to say, the soul by which I am what I am, is entirely distinct from body, and is even more easy to know than is the latter; and even if body were not, the soul would not cease to be what it is."[10]

"What's the point of reading my own words to me?"

She peered down at me over the edge of the book. "Is that thought, *I think, therefore I am*, true?"

"It's true of *me*, yes. *Not* of you."

"I'll ask again: How do you know?"

"You're not conscious."

"Unlike you, you mean?"

"That's right."

"And can you prove that?"

"As I said: only to myself."

"As you said, yes. Let me try a different question. Suppose someone who reads your book does not know whether it was written by a machine or by a man. Would this reader be able to infer, by reading those words, that the proposition, *I think, therefore I am,* is true of the author?"

"No." I shook my head. It was a clever and unexpected question. "Only of the reader."

"You're sure?"

"Yes!"

"Does the word *'I'* in your book refer to the author or the reader?"

"To the author, in the act of writing."

"Then what is proved? To whom is it proved?"

"To myself. As I write."

"Provided you exist, right?"

"But . . ." I rubbed my face, utterly at a loss.

I could recall having had these very thoughts before, in my waking life, but not feeling them so poignantly; philosophy had never mattered to me quite in this way. Mydorge, Villebressieu, Silhon, Mersenne, again their names drifted through my mind, I could hear their voices softly murmuring; ours had been mere intellectual games grounded in abstract questions having to do with scholarly philosophies and conflicting points of view that even in their conflict made us feel comfortable and secure because, regardless of the outcome, they reaffirmed our astuteness, our learned cleverness. Hobbes had once told me, *the guilt of the client only furthers the prestige of the lawyer.* A false position cleverly defended only enhances the philosopher. To falsely first convince yourself and then thinking that you are convinced to further doubly fool the other through thus having fooled yourself seemed to us the very essence of philosophy as it had been taught us by the Jesuits. Now suddenly my very existence, the existence of the world entire, seemed to hang in balance upon the arrangement of the words, the thoughts themselves as if I might somehow fool myself right out of existence. *Self-deception not as self-creation but as philosophical suicide, death by execution. I* was not the prosecutor nor the defense. Nor was I the judge. I was, myself, on trial.

I remembered arguing with Hobbes when he had accused me of plagiarism, of publishing in my *Mediations* nothing new; my arguments, he had claimed, had been better presented before by Augustine and Plato. Though I published his remarks appended to my own work, I had always felt that Hobbes had not understood my true meaning. I had once tried to explain it to him, how Plato's dialogues, which must have seemed but clever fiction to Plato, evolved almost on their own from a philosophical story to become part of the true story of philosophy: the cave which for Plato was but a metaphor to be explained was for us a prison to escape from. In that sense, I had claimed, only half-seriously, Plato had dreamed both Hobbes and me into existence, that Hobbes and I both were but psychological masks who knew not only of Plato's cave but also in what sense we were all cave-dwellers – and not just figuratively but literally. Plato turned a dream into a philosophical vision and gave us existence as selves; Plato's myth transformed itself, through his vision, into modern science. And Augustine, where would he have been were it not for Christ's dream, a dream that could become a vision only when that self ceased to exist in its own confabulation, with Christ's death? And was it not both Christ and Plato who made possible the transcendental vision of

Ramon Llull, who after having five visions tried to write the "best book in the world," which inspired Beeckman and myself, indeed, whose *ars inveniendi veritatem* had transposed into our souls the new foundations for our *mathesis universalis*? I had considered it a great moral victory that Hobbes, the atheist, had on that most apocryphal night in a drunken stupor accused me of blasphemy . . .

A steep wind descended across the ruins, cool and moist and refreshing, as if someone had opened up a window. Looking about the surrounding colonnade glowing eerily with its own effervescence, I saw pitch black clouds rising behind Mt. Parnassus, blotting across the sky like spilled ink, washing out the stars.

Philosophy held out her hand. "Come."

I extended my arm toward her and floated up through the air, effortlessly, ascending gently until our hands touched. Her skin was smooth and warm and inviting. She allowed me to hold her hand as I settled onto the wall next to her. I looked into the intense fiery vacuum of her eyes.

"Your famous 'I think,'" she said. "Let us have a closer look at that."

I thought: what would it be like to kiss her?

"Did you think that thought?"

"Did you hear it?"

"You wondered what it would be like to kiss me," she said, and I realized she could read my thoughts as easily as you can read this book. Her lips swayed, a sorrowful smile. "Well? Did *you* think that thought?"

"Well, I . . . it seems to me I did. Yes. I did think it."

"What makes it seem so?"

I was reminded of her previous question about objects and memories. The objects of perception are ideas that don't look like ideas, they seem external to the mind because they are literally thrown forth before the subject. It is the presence of the subject itself within the mind that makes it possible for the mind to view its own ideas - its own objects - as external to itself. Memories, on the other hand, seem internal because in the memory itself there is no subject and so the image is perceived, correctly, as what it is: a visual phenomenon, a mental image, an idea, an aspect of the self. But memories, like thoughts, don't just appear anywhere, diffused throughout the world of my experience; they seem to arise uniquely from within the self. Thus, the identification of thoughts as being generated by *me,* the self, parallels perfectly the illusion that objects are *not* me - in fact the two illusions are mirror image reversals of each other.

"Looking at my thoughts," I said, hoping to impress her, "I can see that *thinking,* like remembering, appears to be what it is: mental phenomena, *ideas.* Unlike the mental events in this dream that appear to me as objects - you, the ruins - the mental activity of thinking, remembering, feeling, and so on appear as states of mind belonging to the subject. Which suggests, if we were to apply our earlier formula, that I, the subject, am myself no more consciously and directly involved in the act of thinking than I am in the act of constructing these ruins all around me! The existence of thoughts requires the presence of a subject *to which* the thinking is directed, just as the existence objects requires . . . except, again, the strange reversal!" It gave me chills to realize it. "Just as objects belong to my world, thinking belongs to my self. I mean, I hear these very thoughts that I am now saying, just as I hear your side of the dialogue. I *imagine* that I'm consciously composing *these* words in a way that I am not composing yours. I identify completely with this side of the dialogue, I hear this as *me, talking*. But your words, as much as mine, are thoughts! This is a dream. Everything here exists only in my mind, up to and including everything you say. Your side of the dialogue consists of ideas coming at me not as my own thoughts but as the voice of another. Yet *neither* side of the dialogue is *consciously* generated by *me!* This side of the dialogue *feels* like it's the one that is generated by me. But this too is an illusion produced analogously to the way I am able to see my own mental activity not as mental activity but as the ruins of Delphi." I shook my head in disbelief. "I say, 'I'm thinking so and so,' but no more does the subject *think* than the it makes its world, the objects of perception. The self and all its activities, *including thought*, is as much a dream, of purely mental construction, as the world is!"

She reached for a book with a blue and brown cover from the pile on the other side of her and opened it. "'Thinking is not something I do,' she read. 'It is something that happens to me.' Do you recognize those thoughts?"

"I am the author, yes. Why do you keep—"

"Are those *your* thoughts?"

"Yes . . . no! No," I exclaimed, "by my own testimony they are not 'mine.' Thinking is not something *I* do. Right? The 'I' does not initiate thought. The action is not in the

54

subject; thought happens *to* the 'I,' the subject, just as perceptions do, except . . . my God! This is absurd, absolutely preposterous. I've always considered thought – as conceived in linguistic terms, mind you – to be the highest form of mental activity. Now it seems that thinking, by which I mean not the whole sum of mental activity, which is the world entire, but *thinking as it occurs within the self,* belongs not to the higher but the lower . . ."

Philosophy closed the book. I thought I glimpsed someone else's name on the cover but it was too late.

"In that case," she said, "whose thought is that - 'Thinking is not something I do but something that happens to me?'"

"I . . . don't know! Mine, yet not mine? It is . . . my God. *The thinker is Descartes!* The thoughts belong to my self, to Descartes . . . but not to me, the subject. Now you have lost me, completely! If the subject is not the thinking self, who – what – am I?"

She reached for and opened up another book, and read:

> "Now, I realized that not infrequently books speak of books: it is as if they spoke among themselves. In the light of this reflection, the library seemed all the more disturbing to me. It was then the place of long, centuries-old murmuring, an imperceptible dialogue between one parchment and another, a living thing, a receptacle of powers not to be ruled by a human mind, a treasure of secrets emanated by many minds, surviving the death of those who had produced them or had been their conveyors."[11]

She asked, "Recognize the author?"

"Yes! All those are *my . . .*"

Before I completed my sentence and before she could stop me, I pulled from the pile my own *Rules For the Direction of the Mind.* I flipped through it. The words were all there, I could see them with an apparent clarity that in waking life I had never dreamed possible. I saw all the words on the page simultaneously. Every one of them! It made me tremble because I realized that if what I was looking at was accurate, in the dream I could read an entire book in as little time as it took me to flip through the pages. Moreover, the words were not in any language I could identify. They were symbols, but not any symbols I recognized even as I read them, saw them at a glance, understood them! They were the words themselves, the actual words that are the unseen stuff of thought, not their symbolic representations in natural language. It was like being able to see numbers without numerals.

Philosophy took my book from me. Looking at the other books, I saw her pile had a definite boundary and yet I could not tell how many books were in it; it was a small stack but it seemed you could extract any one from an indefinite number of volumes. I reached for a book whose title was *In Search of Myself: Life, Death and Personal Identity* but with a wave of her hand she stopped me. She picked up the scepter and held it in her right hand. I feared my time with her was nearly up, that at any moment the dream would end. The slow curve of the top, I saw, made it a question mark.

"How can I know myself?"

"That question must always remain close at hand."

"Like that scepter that you hold?"

"Like that, yes. Like this," she pointed to the letters sewn into the tight weaves of her fabric, "the Π [pi] and Θ [theta] are the first letters of the Greek words denoting practical and theoretical, and you see them both here upon my robe, in balance." Her smiled sadly. "The scepter is the endless question mark in my left hand without which the endless books in my right are empty tautologies. The question behind your question is the intention behind the imperative that brought you to me: '*Know Your Selves.*'"

"That's not–"

"Yes, it is. The ancient dictum has been transcribed and translated until, finally - unlike your vernacular translation to yourself, 'know yourself,' - it has come to be expressed as 'know thyself.' The imperative has come down through the ages in the formal address, like the French *vous* or the Slavic *vi*, which are plural. The formal address is plural. This is something which modern thought has lost and, in losing it, language has lost the original meaning inscribed on this wall." She pointed downward. "The Oracle speaks, from out of the ruins."

Extending her hand around my shoulder, she gave the slightest pull and we rose and then in slow motion descended toward the ground. I saw the letters that earlier in my waking state (I still thought in such terms) I had touched, ran my index finger along. The symbols were not Greek. They were not French. Nor English. Nor any other any language I could identify; I cannot now as I write this even attempt to draw them. The closest I can do is play some music: Bach comes to mind; but the moment I hear actual music such thoughts make no sense to me, what I am doing makes no sense, for then I hear music and not philosophy; Plato comes to mind: "Philosophy is the highest music."

As we touched ground I was amazed to see the etched words, exactly as before, except now meaning something completely different. I ran my fingers across letters that previously had formed a different sentence. What had changed? Who changed it? Nothing and no one, yet inscribed in the gray stone inside my mind there they were in all their glorious perspicuity, not two words but three:

Know Your Selves.

ENDNOTES

[1] Even as I said it, I saw the problem. To be a subject, which is what I was, meant to *be in the world*, to exist as I was at that moment at the interface between self and other, a fulcrum between Descartes and Delphi. *To be the dreamer* would have required Descartes to exist outside any such coordinate system, beyond himself, an outside without an inside, which is logically impossible. It would have required the "dreaming subject" to be an abstract *universal*, not individual being in space and time, and thereby have deprived the dreamer - as moments ago I had been deprived - of an identity.

[2] Marin Mersenne (1588-1648), a fellow pupil with Descartes at La Flèche and his best friend. He went on to become such a celebrated mathematician ("Mersenne numbers" are named after him) and theologian that the British philosopher Thomas Hobbes (1588-1679) remarked that of his vast knowledge "there was more than in all the universities together." He not only acted as intermediary between Descartes and many other philosophers of the time but collected the various objections to Descartes' Meditations that were published, with Descartes' replies, as an appendix to that immortal work.

[3] The self is the body, it is (what in theory I would call) the body image (in space) exclusively conjoined to the mind image (in time), the ego. The subject is - to use her words - the fulcrum of consciousness, it is the nonexistent head.

[4] The categories of memory in that sense determine the categories of reality.

[5] Does this beg the question against materialism? Interestingly enough, the 'materialist' position has changed drastically over the past several centuries. Materialists used to argue, when rather naïve theories of perception were in vogue, that the objects in perception had to a certain degree their qualities structured by the physical structure of the external objects of which they were representations. It was thought at the time that there was a direct causal correspondence

between the external object in the world 'out there,' the object perceived, and the mind's representation of it, the perceived object. The perception of objects in dreams is an obvious counter-example that should have already alerted those early materialists but didn't. When it turned out that such theories were seriously flawed for many reasons, such as that any material reconstruction of perception involved active processing on the part of the brain that was functionally completely independent of the external world, so much so that any 'direct' causal affectation of the objects in experience by their external counterparts was out of the question, materialism became an altogether different doctrine regarding the nature of perception, having to do with an elaborate neurological approach in which dreams are not so obviously a counter-example. But the point here is that even if dream objects are representations that turn out to be physically reducible to brain states, the perceived stability and permanence is not itself derived from the nature of the 'permanence' of the underlying physical substance in which the dream objects consist. Neurons actively fire, the structuring of perceptions by a neural network requires much active processing, and so on. In other words, it is not the 'stability' of that of which the perceived objects are representations (possible objects? imaginary objects?) that accounts for the perceived structure! Scientific 'realism' and naïve 'realism' have nothing in common but the word; even upon the crudest reflection scientific realism must deny and undermine naïve realism as surely as the most blatant form of idealism does.

6 And why not? Because, ultimately, I believed that physical objects cannot so easily pass through each other. And why did I believe this? Because I have had experiences of rigid objects. But were the rigid objects of my experience, themselves, physical objects? No – they were the objects of my experience, events in the mind. So how did I know what I thought I knew about the nature and behavior of physical objects? Because of an inference based on the nature and behavior of mental objects. But what made me infer the

existence of the physical in the first place? The peculiar nature of the mental objects. And why did I find their nature peculiar? Because they showed permanence, resilience, rigidity, and so on. And I believed that this is *not* how mental objects, themselves behave – but why did I believe that? Why, especially, when dreams showed me that the permanence, resilience, and rigidity could be experienced without any underlying physical objects being the cause of any such representations? Experience itself teaches me what experience, as a mental phenomenon, can do, how fixed and rigid it can be in and of itself. And it is only on the bases of it that I can venture to extrapolate about the nature of things beyond experience. But what then would be the motive? Not explanation. Something else. What? Deception.

[7] Why do I say, whether in a dream or waking state? Because when I am awake I am asleep to the fact that to be perceived an object requires a perceiving subject, that this is itself a mental process, regardless of the ultimate nature of the universe. Asleep, I am awake! Awake, I am asleep.

[8] See note 11.

[9] How does mind interact with mind? Self-consciousness conceived in its 'pure' form is empty, like logic: it has the structure of space. Perhaps it's power lies in its very powerlessness to retain content and structure, to be completely transformed by its surrounding content, and to thereby impose formal relations on any content applied to it. The conscious mind could thus be conceived as an amorphous being, a metaphysical chameleon, an entity that can transform itself into any world, any self; *I* can be anything and anyone because I am no one, an empty space, a nothing.

[10] Descartes, *The Philosophical Works*, trans. Elizabeth S. Haldane and G.R.T. Ross (Cambridge: Cambridge Univ. Press 1931), I, 101.

[11] Umberto Eco, quoted in John Barrow and Frank Tipler, The Anthropic Cosmological Principle, New York: Oxford University Press 1988.

THREE:

MEMORIES

OF

AMNESIA

Behind your thoughts and feelings, my brother, there stands a mighty ruler, an unknown sage - whose name is self.

Friedrich Nietzsche

I AWOKE FLAT ON MY BACK, TUCKED INSIDE my sleeping bag, staring straight up into an iridescent black velvet sky spewn with stars. I sat up; cold sweat rolled down my face and back. The moon was just setting into Mt. Parnassus, its golden yellow curved question mark sizzling through the pines.

My arms and legs tingled as if my entire body had fallen asleep. The ringing in my ears sounded like static. I stood up in the frosty darkness and walked to the wall atop which Philosophy had just been sitting, half expecting her to be there. Everything looked exactly as it had during the dream and I could not be certain, as I stumbled through the open doorway, whether I was now awake or still dreaming. On the other side of the wall where, it seemed but moments ago, I had been standing, I found the inscription in the original Greek letters, which I now read, without having to consciously think it, as *"Know Your Selves."*

Back inside the temple I lit a candle and placed it in a corner where the wind would not blow it out. I took out a blank notebook and with trembling hands began to write:

> I just woke up from a dream in which I dreamt
> I was Descartes . . .

Later I would reorganize my notes into a chronological narrative. Now I wrote like a madman, scribbling wildly, jotting down anything and everything I could think of . . . suddenly, I stopped. I could feel the surface of my skin (skin? is this my *skin*? is this *my* skin?), the tightening of gooseflesh, dread of I knew not what, wrinkling itself across my soul. Shivering, I took off my T-shirt and jeans. I wiped myself with the shirt and tossed it onto the rock to dry until morning. I put on my sweat suit. The clean cotton, washed and dried in the sun, felt like soft gauze against my trembling skin. And suddenly I was fine again.

What was the matter with me? I must have caught a chill .

. . the phrase echoed through the labyrinth of my mind: *caught a chill*. It was but the shadow of a memory, as if my body was remembering having been someone other than myself: *Descartes* had caught a chill. Somewhere within me something had expected to find itself in an unhealthy and perhaps dying body . . . but what - who? And as I thought about it I wondered: *when did I become Kolak?* It chilled me to see how carelessly I had written that first sentence into my notebook. I began once again to write, feeling this time as if I were possessed by a daemon.

Soon the entire notebook was filled. The candle had burned nearly all the way down. I closed the notebook and returned it to my knapsack. Leaning forward to blow the candle out, I noticed the jagged pattern of the melted wax. There was no particular shape to it, just a coagulated blob, but it too leaped out at me, a déjà vu of having seen that shape before exactly as now, when I had ruminated - no, when *Descartes* had so famously ruminated, in his *Meditations,* about the piece of candle wax. *Some part of me must still be in the grip of the dream,* I rationalized. That's exactly the way the thought presented itself to me, (mis)identifying me as the perceiving subject of that memory. It was, I told myself (and I had to tell myself, as if to censor and snuff by thought the 'magical' feeling that I really was Descartes), merely the remnant of a dream.

Yet still I felt as if I had just been him – as if I hadn't dreamt I was Descartes but had been Descartes. I felt emotionally disoriented, fearful but in a strange way. Usually when you're frightened of something you want to escape from it. I had no desire to escape, I did not want to be free of the memory of having been someone else, of having been *him*, the founder of modern philosophy, the strangeness of it. I would have traded a thousand days of my waking life for another such dream; a thousand such dreams swapped for the remaining waking days of my life I might have gladly accepted, without hesitation.

Suddenly the goose bumps and chills returned: *I can't imagine what that would be like, to be anyone other than Descartes. But I see it could be possible. Except I think I would be much surprised to find myself believing, with this feeling of certainty, that I was someone else . . .* My own words – or were they *his?* – came back to haunt me, my dialogue with Philosophy struck me now in an entirely different way: *Who would be surprised? If you woke up to find you were 'someone else' other than Descartes, would it be Descartes who was 'someone else?'*

No, of course not. It would be me, who in this dream falsely remembers himself as Descartes, who upon waking would remember himself as . . . whoever.

And who is that?

I remembered the feeling of certainty that I was Descartes, a feeling that no amount of thinking could dispel: *Would I be surprised at finding myself attached, as it were, to a different world through a 'different' mask, other than the one I am now in this dream? No! For what I would then be surprised by - perhaps even rightly disturbed - would be the recollection of having ever believed I was Descartes.* Surprised, indeed! And the most remarkable thing about it was that the person I *tried* to convince myself in the dream that I was – Mersenne – thinking this was at least the most plausible among a slew of implausibilties, now seemed utterly the most implausible and absurd example. The 'truth' that 'I' was 'Kolak' had not even been an option.

Indeed, I could barely fathom the fact that only moments ago all my *present* memories – up to and including, *my own name - had been utterly unknown to me!* Yet that was *me, I* was there! I remembered vividly picking up the copy of *In Search of Myself,* a name that should have been familiar to me for it was the working title of the manuscript in my knapsack, a manuscript I had been working on during my travels. The idea then that I was who I *now* am had seemed so utterly preposterous to me I could not imagine it, much less believe it, yet there I was now, fixed in the belief that I was a student named Daniel Kolak backpacking through Greece.

I wondered what had enabled me to think such thoughts in the dream. How could I who knew so little about philosophy suddenly seem to know so much, with such authority, about so many things, and all this knowledge seemed to have come entirely from within me . . . I began to feel agitated, physically as well as mentally, as if my head was on fire. Such things were impossible, I knew they were. *Suppose in your previous life you were Descartes?* What if coming to the temple had stoked the memories from my soul and the dream was what it seemed to be, a recollection of a past life, as in the regressive hypnotherapies that I had read about and heard my professors debunk, in which people under hypnosis seem to remember events from past lives? It seemed preposterous, utterly ridiculous, insane . . .

All right, just get a hold of yourself. It was just a dream, a very vivid dream. Stuff like that happens. The details you either picked up from somewhere or your brain confabulated them. You've heard of crazier things. This is a great learning experience, that's all, crazy but enlightening. Work it into your book, make it part of the story. It just may turn out to be the greatest learning experience you've ever had . . .

My thoughts turned to Philosophy's "Know Your *Selves*." A new meaning to an ancient phrase. I wondered at how a dream - indeed, a dream character in a dream (for surely that's all she was) - could change the meaning of a phrase that had come to be so familiar. I had heard that phrase many times and never had I thought to reinterpret it. Likewise with what the 'Goddess of Wisdom' (the phrase now made me smile) had 'taught' me. It wasn't so much that the ideas were completely new to me (though in many cases they were). Much of what Philosophy had said I had heard in lectures, or had read about. Rather, it was as if the dream provided a context in which the ideas freshly and freely, without any 'steering' from me, reinterpreted themselves not *by* me but *through* me, nourished and nourishing, coming to life within me. By comparison I felt I had been sleepwalking through all those years of college, embalming ideas with my intellect rather than allowing myself to be brought to life by them. To become Descartes within myself I had become entirely dead to Kolak. Did one have to die like that, I wondered, in order to be born? I thought of Socrates, of all the great poets' love affairs with death while living, of the eastern sages espousing

67

the ending within one's self of the known to make room for
the unknown, of the may lovers of wisdom whom I loved and
in doing so had betrayed wisdom. Wisdom betrayed by the
love of her lovers! I wrote that down, too, self-amused by the
clever but mannered turn of phrase, attending to my own
cleverness in my own typical egotistical fashion. I was Kolak all
right. And in that moment of self-criticism I realized, in a flash
of insight, that self-criticism too was no less egotistical than
self-aggrandizement, no less vein, no less false and illusory . . .

I began trembling again. I lay back down in my sleeping
bag in exactly the same position I had been lying in during the
dream. There was a dull pain on my left side. I felt frightened,
stupid, irrational, alone. Without question I now fully
accepted without question (that is, in the purely verbal,
intellectual sense) that the world I was in was real, that the
world in which I now perceived myself to be lying down in the
sleeping bag was not a dream. The effortlessness of my
thinking in the dream was gone. But why? How did I even
know I was not still dreaming? Because Philosophy was not
there? Because, I reassured myself, I was not the father of
modern philosophy but a young man at the tail end of the
twentieth century who had just dreamt he was Descartes? But,
first, where had I - Kolak - been while I had dreamt I was
Descartes? As Descartes I had had no Kolak memories
whatsoever. I did not even behave or talk like Kolak. So in
what sense had that been Kolak dreaming he was Descartes?
Did *I* and *Kolak really* have different referents?

I tried to compare my present 'waking state' of
consciousness with my 'dream state' of consciousness. Could I

see any difference? No, I could not. *You're not looking,* I heard Philosophy's voice inside me say. So then I realized the following question:[1] how did I know that *that* had been 'the most vivid' dream I had ever had? I quickly leafed through my notebook; page after page, there it was, throughout the entire 'transcription' of my convoluted conversations with Philosophy: the assertion about it having been 'the most vivid' dream I had ever had was *in the text* but *not* in my *consciousness*, not in my memory. Any past state remembered will always look less realistic that the present state of remembering; hadn't I learned in the dream that I can have no direct access to any but my present states of consciousness? So how then did I know that the dream was as vivid as my present state of consciousness? Again I looked at my memories (not words, not texts, but *images)* from the dream. I remembered the scene in which Philosophy had glided down off the wall. I replayed the scene in my mind . . . *the scene.* I had remembered and yet, in my remembering had forgotten: memory consists of scenes, dim translucent images – *not* objects.

I looked at the wall in front of me. I had no way of judging whether this wall was any more or less 'realistic' than the wall experienced as an object in my dream. I ran my hand along it and remembered in the dream trying to put my hand through it; again I did the same and the objects - the hand and wall - behaved in my 'waking' state exactly as they had behaved in the dream. This was so simple, so obvious, so incredible and it absolutely startled me. Even more incredible was the fact that I now fully realized that I had no way whatsoever for ascertaining in consciousness what I had only moments ago stated to myself to be true and had even written down: that dream and waking states were indistinguishable. Yet I knew now and believed in the phenomenological indistinguishability of dream and waking states. So how, then, did I know this?

The answer was in the book in front of me. The way I knew it, if at all, was through the arrangement of the words themselves. Not by experience, which is a dream, but by Philosophy's argument. Such knowledge (perhaps all knowledge) is, literally, textual. In that moment of lucidity I asked myself what words are, then, if not windows into dreams, into other worlds? I wrote down this strange phrase:

Eyes are not windows. Words are.

I got up. I reminded myself (and used neither experience nor reason nor even consciousness, for you cannot use them) to remind myself: *this is still a dream even though you are awake.* I am awake. I am dreaming. It is the words themselves that enlighten. The right words, arranged properly in sequence like opening a lock, or like the notes of a chord that open up your heart to something. And yet somehow within me I felt as if I knew, discordantly, that now I was *not* dreaming, just as during the dream I had felt as if I knew I was dreaming - just as in the dream I had thought I knew I was Descartes and as now in my waking state I thought I knew I was Kolak! Philosophy's argument about thoughts and sensations came back to me with added force: the sensation of believing you were awake and the sensation of believing you were sleeping are both out of your control, that is, beyond the control of the subject, beyond reach of self and all your conscious mental

70

states except to read them. They are like ROM (Read Only Memory) of a computer. I, at least insofar as I am a conscious being, aware of my existence over time, am no more the cause of the thoughts and sensations being experienced by me at any particular moment than I am the cause of my perceptions. Right now as I write this in front of me I see a computer, the notebooks I brought back from Delphi (which, I am amazed, contain so many of these words) pictures I took with my camera; I consciously do nothing to see these items, they are ready-made for me (I believe) by some aspect of my mind or brain, processes beyond reach of consciousness. I cannot, even now as I write and rewrite these words, reach back into the inner workings of my mind and brain to see how this, what is here being seen and said, comes into existence as a melange of objects properly arranged in perception and thought to produce exactly such and such a state to make experience possible. My whole world seems as thoroughly prefabricated, ready-made, and inaccessible to consciousness as ROM memory is to re-recording by the viewer, as this book is to rewriting by you, the reader, as if my world were an already finished book, playing itself out, being read . . .

So much to think about - but am *I* even thinking? No. *Thinking is happening,* I heard both the question and the answer as one hears a voice, privy to whispers from within, remembering the words of Ludwig Wittgenstein - which in the dream I had 'recognized' as my own! I had only recently completed a seminar on Wittgenstein and his writings had had made *no sense whatsoever* to me: "Thinking is not something I do, but something that happens to me."[2] Now I understood and was amazed. Even the phrase *the subject,* which was littered throughout philosophy, *had been completely passed over by me, the subject!* I had thought I understood but now I realized the words had meant almost nothing to me by comparison to what they now meant. Indeed, all those longwinded discussions about perception, experience, knowledge, dream and reality, God and free will, which intrigued and amused me, suddenly seemed profound beyond belief! Even the workings of my own mind, which I always had taken for granted, were open to me in an utterly new way, up to and including the activity of *thinking.*

Thinking is not something I do. I can try to influence 'my' thoughts in one of two ways. I can either, on the one hand, accept or reject them or, on the other, ask questions of myself (or not). But that too is an illusion! Paying now careful attention to the impetus of such acceptances, rejections, and questions as they are perceived by me, the subject, I see that these states of consciousness simply fall into consciousness like rain falls from the sky. So do the insights fall which layer themselves throughout this process; I am not even an observer, a watcher, for my attention itself is not an activity of which I am the cause: attention too, like all 'my' sensations, emotions and thoughts, is more like the way wind blows the falling rain. The wind does not cause rain to fall but only, at most, diverts it just a little, while its own direction, where the wind blows to and from, is not the wind's own doing. Nothing in consciousness is *my* doing. Whose, then?

Perhaps no one's. I knew that's what David Hume and Gautama Buddha had taught. I knew so many things, it seemed, and yet all I wanted to do was to go back into a dream state to converse again with Philosophy - to talk to myself in a dream within a dream! (Was that desire itself part of the program? It seemed not. But I knew - or, should I say, the words themselves knew – that nothing is what it seems.) I cared more of what an imaginary being, Philosophy, might go on to say about such things than I cared what I myself or any other 'real' being consciously thought or said. (Caring, too, and what matters - values themselves - everything suddenly seemed a readymade thing, paint-by-numbers thinking, stillborn, fixed into the grooves of thought, completely dead.)

Again, I was no stranger to these thoughts and questions, these dilemmas, these paradoxical labyrinths of inquiry into self, knowledge, reality, freedom, and God. But now I found myself wondering anew: what did *I* believe, and did it matter? Was there room in all this cognitive machinery for a living, breathing, conscious being as I had always seemed - no, not *seemed*, for the subject does not seem - to be: a pointing away, within the world, from everything that could be pointed at in the world? (Didn't Wittgenstein say something like that?)

I lay there on my sleeping bag, trying but failing to go to sleep, mulling over the sudden poignancy of that question whose full impetus I had never before felt: what did *I* believe? For it had seemed to me, up until that dream, that philosophy was a sort of metaphysical map for getting wherever you wanted to go. What did I believe - Maine or Florida? Wrong question! I know how to get you to Maine provided you know where you are; if you are in New York, go north. If you are in Alaska, go South. Likewise, I know how to get you to Florida;

if in New York, go south. What about California? If in New York, go west. So what about me, which way do *I* go? Whenever friends of fellow students would ask me what I believed that is exactly how I felt: they were asking the wrong question. I could tell you how to get wherever you wanted to go, provided you knew where you were. Clearly, and this always amused me, most people did not even know that. Once you knew where you were, then I could help you find a good intellectual travel agent to wherever you wanted to go: Berkeley, Hume, Russell, Buddha, Plato, Aristotle, Kant, Hegel, Descartes . . . what's your pleasure, your preferred destination? The great lovers of wisdom were like so many great places to me; wonderful, exotic places. Unlike most of my fellow students, the question of which philosophy was the true one, the correct one, the best one, never seemed important. Sentences are true or false, not arguments; sentences are valid or invalid: philosophies are worlds of discourse within which certain sentences and arguments fit, as such, into a conceptual scheme, while others do not. To me, there were, and still are, an infinite number of philosophical worlds. Philosophy itself meant that to me. When you know what philosophy is that's what you know. It isn't relativism or skepticism. It is, rather, a multi-perspectival vision, an intellectual map of the conceptual universe.

Anyway, that's sort of where (and who) I was up to the point at which I had arrived at Delphi, fresh out of college. I had come there seeking I knew not what, something 'profound' - a connection, perhaps, through ancient roots back to myself. But even in my loftiest thoughts I had never

74

expected anything quite like *Descartes among the ruins.*

I crawled inside the cover of my sleeping bag and leaned back onto the cool fabric. I folded my arms across my chest and waited. I felt a strange sense of relief, of completion, while at the same time feeling anxious, a great anticipation. I wasn't so much hoping for another dream as expecting it. When it didn't come I - strange though this now strikes me - forgot all about it. (How can you forget a dream like that, even for a moment?) I lay there, staring into space. My eyes had found a star to rest on, a blazing white sun light years away. It felt good to be lying down and staring up like that, listening to the swelling rhythms of the cicadas. A tree frog, probably there in that young cypress just beyond the first colonnade, added a poignant timber to the cacophony.

With the moon now gone (having set for the second time that night!) the stars shone even brighter. I traced the Milky Way. I could see perfectly clearly the swelling bulge of the center of our galaxy. Back home in Massachusetts the sky is flat; here, as I had seen it when I sailed across the Atlantic, the sky is a curved dome of luminous darkness spewing star shadows onto the Earth below. I remembered the words of a pop song: "*Ma chéri amour,* as distant as the Milky Way." The line is either incredibly dumb or incredibly brilliant; the distance to the Milky Way is no distance at all, it is all around you. You're already there, here and now, in the Milky Way.

I returned again to thinking about my thoughts. Where had that thought, the line from the possibly profound pop song, come from? I had not consciously sifted through some storehouse of melodies. The pop song had just popped into

75

my head! Like the next thought after that. In neither case did I myself consciously do anything to remember. I could have gone on to something else but didn't. And this thought - the thought that I did nothing consciously to initiate either of the thoughts above - where did *it* come from? *This* thought seemed to be chasing *that* one, or running away from some other one, but it is not *I* who chases or runs . . .

I thus kept watch (though this too is not something *I* did but merely something that, I now noted, happened to me) on my own thoughts dancing about inside my head, popping in and out of the void, needing the void to exist, like the star I was looking at needed and breeded the void around itself.

My thoughts soon returned again, like pigeons to a perch, to that new ancient proposition, *know your selves.* What does this new interpretation of an old saying 'really' mean? "I" implies something that is numerically one. *Selves* implies the opposite. Was *I,* myself a many? "I am large," wrote Walt Whitman in *Song of Myself,* "I contain multitudes." There is also the possibility of multiplicity over time. How, for instance, did I know that I, the awake person lying there on my back staring up at the sky, am one and the same *I* who was sitting up on that wall, talking to Philosophy? By *memory?* But memory divides much more than it connects: it is, as Philosophy had taught me, the dividing wall of inner space, out of which the self is constructed, as language itself is . . .

I remembered writing down the thought, "I dreamt I was Descartes." But *who* dreamt *who* was *who?* Well, I remember that dialogue between Philosophy and Descartes, I remember witnessing the conversation from the first person point of view. That is all. That dream character thought he was a Frenchman living in Stockholm, Sweden, I think I am a Frenchman living in the U.S.; he thought he graduated from La Flèche, I think I graduated from Harvard, and so on. But, I knew, memory is neither sufficient nor necessary for personal identity. Suppose instead of remembering that dream I had forgotten it; often, and usually, we forget our dreams. All that would still have happened to *me* - wouldn't it have? Or, suppose I'm not a graduate of Harvard but, say, the University of Maryland. Didn't that dream still happen to me? (and then, I had the strangest thought: what if I am wrong even about *that*, or even *more* - what if this, now, is really Descartes dreaming he is Kolak? A crazy thought!) And if I didn't graduate from Harvard but Maryland, or someplace else, am I not in either case the same person? But who, then, am *I*, the one to whom these thoughts happen? What makes *me* the same *I* from one situation to the next?

Round and round it went around in my head like that, it seemed for hours. The problem of identity at a time loomed just as large. Are there other conscious selves within my mind right now, conscious centers of first-person points of view with which *I* - *this* subject - am not co-conscious? It was all just so many words to me now, devoid of much significance (except, perhaps, as some sort of philosophical poetry). Or, is there some super-*I*, over and above this lower I, a sort of transcendental self - perhaps, even, the *metaphysical subject* (whatever *that* might be!)? (But what would its metaphysical *objects* be? Another absurd idea!)

Suddenly, without realizing it, I was looking not up at the

77

star but down at it. I was still lying flat on my back - I could feel the silky texture of the sleeping bag, the pressure of my head against the goose down - but it was as if I was strapped with my back to a ceiling, as if the Earth at my back was the ceiling of the universe and the entire cosmos a deep dark well that I was falling into, a bottomless pit of unfixed stars. I had heard once an astronaut describe such things happening in outer space, between the Earth and Moon, even in Earth orbit; suddenly you lose all sense of up and down or it becomes reversed and you feel crazy and you never tell Houston about it if ever again you want to fly.

I didn't dare move. Lying there, petrified, feeling my heart pounding in my chest, I thought I was having a heart attack or a seizure or maybe dying. I had trouble breathing, as if inside and outside had somehow been reversed in me so that now I had to exhale to inhale. Is this what a heart attack feels like, I wondered, how death comes, with loss of breath spreading outward, with complete loss of control? At that moment my thoughts of only a few moments ago about consciousness and personal identity seemed utterly moot. All the humor and cleverness vanished from the situation and I just wanted to *be*, to continue to exist. *I don't care who I am. Just let me be, please, . . .*

"Get up." I heard Philosophy's soft voice.

A chill shook me. "Where are you? I can't see you—"

"Here. Look up. Here I am."

I lifted my head; actually, I lowered my chin. Philosophy stood in the open doorway of the temple, silhouetted against the softly glowing ruins of the colonnade behind her. She lay her books on the threshold and leaned the scepter against the doorway. She looked angry.

As soon as I sat up the sensation of hanging upside down vanished. "What *was* that!"

"What did it feel like?"

"Complete loss of control, horrible . . . *why?*"

"Why the loss of control, or why the horror?" Her matter-of-factness seemed somehow to put me at ease.

"Both," I said. "I was lying there, thinking about my dream . . . I mean, my God, Descartes' world - *that* whole world, the one I then imagined was my one and only real world - how could I have made up all those memories, those details, the people? How could I have invented that whole reality? I seemed to remember whole conversations with people who don't exist - names and places and all manner of details which I don't know anything about and couldn't possibly know anything about . . . anyway, thinking about it I must have fallen asleep without noticing-"

"What makes you think you were awake?"

"Wasn't I?"

"Oh, Daniel - shall I call you Daniel?"

"Call me Ishmael," I said and tried to make myself laugh but it gave me shivers to realize *I now believed I was Daniel Kolak with less certainty than in the first dream I had believed I was Descartes!* I could feel the empty tingling feeling tickling my insides like a tightly coiled spring, ready at any time to snap me in half . . .

"Listen," I said, "the body in that sleeping bag, in which I . . . in which the dreamer . . . the body . . . I don't know what

79

to call that! That object is . . . a what?"

"Can there be an object without a subject?"

"I know, but–"

"To what object, then, are you referring?" She pointed to the sleeping bag. *"That* object in *that* bag?"

"No, of course, there is no object in *that* bag. *That* bag is empty! I mean the object of which this headless body I am in is a representation."

She shook her head disdainfully. "Suppose all this exists through the fiction of someone else's imagination. In that case *Kolak*, the self through which you presently view yourself and the world, *does not exist.* Nothing resembling anything like the ruins you see here before you exists. Is this possible?"

"No."

"Just as it was impossible, in the earlier dream, for you to conceive how you could be someone other than Descartes? Don't play games! Could you have imagined then that what you are experiencing now was possible, that anything like this would ever come to pass? When you were asking me *then* about your body, the body you imagined asleep in Stockholm . . . *is it possible that the body you now conceive as the container of this dream is as unreal as that other body was in your earlier dream?"*

I was trembling. "It's possible."

"Come." She extended her hand through the doorway. "What then would that 'object' of which you claim your body is a representation - Kolak's body - *be?"*

"No object at all."

She took her books and scepter and together we left the

80

temple. "What, then?"

"An imaginary . . . purely . . . imaginary object? No. Not *object*, because no subject, no first person point of view as such, is involved. And not *imaginary* because there is no image involved except in a funny reversal, in which one tries to . . . I don't know what to call it!"

"You see? When you think of 'objects' out there beyond your mind that the objects you perceive represent, you use the 'representations' themselves as the source for the thing-in-itself. Which is completely circular! But nor is the thing in itself supposedly referred to in this way an *imaginary* object, because no image as such is associated with it. These ruins, for instance, which you take to be images of the 'real' ones outside your head: if any image you see as an object presently before you does not actually have any corresponding thing out there of which it is a representation, then the 'thing' is a . . . what? To what are you referring, when you think of perceptions as representations? What do you believe the objects in this dream would be if there were no ruins as such of which these were a representation and no Kolak – *exactly in the way you now believe was true in the corresponding situation when you believed, with all credulity, that you were Descartes asleep in Stockholm? Where is your bedroom now? Where is Stockholm now?*"

"I . . . don't know!" I gripped the sides of my arms. "These objects here exist for me regardless of whether they are accurate or inaccurate representations, or not even representations but merely presentations that do not represent anything. When I think of things-in-themselves I think of . . .

what? Theoretical objects?"

"Perhaps, if there is a theory associated with their existence, yes; otherwise not."

"Otherwise *what?* Fictions?"

"Nothing," she said. "They refer to nothing at all. The words are empty."

I felt suddenly very cold. We exited the first colonnade and continued walking slowly up the incline toward the Apollo theater.

"I must now ask you a question," she said, "one you intuited earlier when you wondered about what you perceive dreams with. The problem, I want you to see, is much deeper: what do you *ever* perceive *anything* with? How are appearances, your own mental states, ever apprehended? Not with your eyes, for when you dream your eyes are closed. For you, the subject - identified here in the dream as that self, Kolak, situated atop what you see as a headless dream body - have *what* for eyes? What do you, the perceiving subject, perceive me - or any other - objects, with?"

"I don't know!" I placed my hand next to my eyes, fingers pointing at myself. "These are not my eyes." I could see the fingertips. "These blurry fingertips I see pointing at myself are part of this embodied self, my dream body, but what they are being seen with I have no idea. How can I answer, when there is not even a word for that - is there? For in a dream I have *no eyes.*"

She pulled me out into the open courtyard. The cool dry breeze, blowing gently from all directions, rippled her gown against her body. I took her arm again, feeling her voluptuous

82

warmth. We reached the end of the second colonnade where a row of shrubs with oleander flowers and sword plants divided the temple from the theater. She handed me a book and with the same motion opened it. Again there were those dizzying symbols which seemed directly to speak with the voice of my own thoughts, a dazzle of impossibility. I wish I could draw or even remember them. But all I have are the words from Plato's *Republic*, which as she read them I understood for the first time:

> "The many, as we say, are seen but not known, and the ideas are known but not seen. . . . Noble, then is the bond which links together sight and visibility, and great beyond other bonds by no small difference of nature; for light is their bond, and light is no ignoble thing. . . . Whose is that light which makes the eye to see perfectly and the visible to appear? . . . Yet of all the organs of sense the eye is the most like the sun . . . and the soul is like the eye."[3]

"I've read that before," I said, "but never realized Plato's point about the eye being like the sun! He's asking about *the eye of the soul*, isn't he? When I think of seeing, I think of light bouncing off an object - one of those subjectless, 'objective objects' so popular in physical theory - and then striking the eye, which is like a receiving antenna that then transmits information taken from the light to the brain, where it is used to construct a visual representation of the object. But what is perceived in this or any other moment, by the subject are objects that, as such, cannot be perceived by 'subjectless' objects – physical eyes, brains, bodies, etc., - but *only* by the subject. Common sense ignores this. It says that the objects one is looking at radiate *from* the objects one sees *to* the point where one seems to find oneself located. And that's not the case. Such a state of affairs makes no sense once I understand myself to exist but inside my own dream world. Right?"

"Go on," she said.

"Well, what I think you have taught me is that I am myself but an idea in the mind that, as such, doesn't need to go through some sort of lens in order to be transmitted to a brain! Indeed, ideas *cannot* be thus transmitted. Ideas are, already, *in* the brain, if there is a brain (or else nowhere and a type of nothing). It is *I,* the subject, who actualizes the objects in my world as such. Without a mind to first process the . . . information? Text? 0's and 1's, whatever there is - there would be no object-subject relation. So any objects I am looking at are not themselves the source of their own presence. Rather, it is the mind's eye, the subject - whatever that might be (but clearly it is not a psychological or physiological eye for it is nowhere seen) - that generates them." I paused. "This means that what we have been calling the subject - this 'psychological location' within this dream experience, the topological point that I am – this itself is part of the *generator* of these objects, not their *receiver.* Right?" How odd, I thought: *I'm trying to impress her with what a good student I can be. Why?* "Which means I don't so much *see* you as *project* you?"

She grinned. "Now your thinking almost reaches the nineteenth century!" She laughed seductively, insultingly.

"You are making progress, Ishmael–"

"Wait a minute," I said. "In our earlier discussion, it seemed the point was that I was only a *passive* receiver of images, thoughts, sensations . . . now it seems I have concluded just the opposite." It made me laugh to realize the impossible coherence, the tracking, of this unfolding dream play, this philosophical drama. "I, as the subject, located at a particular place in my world - in this, what presently appears to me as my immediately surrounding space of objects - am not an *observer* viewing. I am *the* viewing?"

"Restate this, please!"

"How easy it is to slip into waking prejudice! I, the subject, am not an observer viewing these objects. I – the subject - am their . . . *actualizer?*"

"Be more careful still. Are you *subject only?*"

"No! I had, only a moment ago, realized this but then immediately forgot: *I am subject and I am object.* But wait! Although I am myself involved in this way from both sides in my world, as self and other, the objects perceived in my world are themselves projected into it through me, the subject. So in that sense - just as I am not the viewer of the world but the viewing - I am also not the generator of the world; I am the generation. I am in that sense not an object but a function." I paused. *"I* am the actualizer of my world?"

"Without you there is no world, that's right."

"All this in a strange way seems ultimately to reinforce my earlier realization - namely, that what *I* am is the *seeing itself,* though not in any consciously active sense. The subject is like a two-way lens; the perceived objects - all these presently actual objects - come into my world in this present moment (which I know to be but a dream) through the subject and they in the same instant are comprehended and brought into consciousness through the subject. The subject is like a lens that is at the same time projector and camera . . . you know, I think I've finally understood idealism! I mean, absolute, idealism! Berkeley, Fichte, Hegel, Schelling, Schopenhauer, Royce, none of them made any sense to me before. Back at Harvard they made me wonder how such great figures could ever have had such absolutely crazy thoughts!"

"Who made you?"

"My professors! But you see now I finally understand what all those great philosophers are saying! It's never been clear to me before how the self could somehow be involved in the actualization of the world, in making existence actual. Even your earlier remarks about the passive nature of the *I*, though I now realize I never properly understood that either, seemed wrongheaded and unpersuasive to me, I mean, you know, to Descartes – I mean–"

"I understand." Smiling, Philosophy opened a book and began reading from the beginning of Schopenhauer's *World as Will and Idea*:

> "'The world is my idea' is, like the axioms of Euclid, a proposition which everyone must recognize as true as soon as he understands it, although it is not a proposition that everyone understands as soon as he hears it. . . . among the many things that make the world so puzzling and precarious, the first and foremost is that, however

immeasurable and massive it may be, its existence hangs nevertheless on a single thread; and this thread is the actual consciousness in which it exists. This condition, with which the existence of the world is irrevocably encumbered, marks it with the stamp of ideality, in spite of all empirical reality, and consequently with the stamp of the mere phenomenon. Thus the world must be recognized, from one aspect at least, as akin to a dream. For the same brain-function that conjures up during sleep a perfectly objective, perceptible, and indeed palpable world must have just as large a share in the presentation of the objective world of wakefulness. . . . the two worlds are nevertheless obviously molded from one form. This form is the intellect, the brain-function. Descartes was probably the first to attain the degree of reflection demanded by that fundamental truth; consequently, he made that truth the starting point of his philosophy . . ."[4]

"I understand perfectly," I said, "how this is true right now within this dream. But you know what? This dream, albeit a very unusual and vivid one, makes such thoughts so visceral an experience that I don't even care whether what Schopenhauer and the other idealists are saying about the world entire applies to everything that exists in any realm whatsoever or just to these psychological states within this dream and to me. I want merely to understand how this is possible even at this local, immediate, vivid, incontrovertible level. How dare philosophers today even proceed without first addressing this problem! For I know both that it *is* so at this dream level and that I do not know *how* it could be so. Furthermore, it seems in my quest to know myself I have stumbled upon the role of the subject that is both exactly passive in the way common sense supposes the subject is active, and active in exactly the way that common sense supposes the subject to be passive! What a complete metaphysical reversal! I have never so clearly, distinctly, and downright simply seen this double falseness with regard to our ordinary, waking conception of ourselves."

"Quite so," said Philosophy. "No doubt you now wonder how far your present insights reach beyond the dream and apply to what you call the 'real' world. Right?"

"I'm sorry. Yes. I can't help it."

"Put it in the form of a question."

"I . . . can't."

We stood very close. I detected a little smile at the corner of her lips. She threw me a provocative sideways glance.

"Then I will repeat *my* question," she said. "Given everything that has thus far been said, how would you distinguish, now, the world in which you presently find yourself, from the world in which you find yourself in what you call your 'waking' states?"

"Ah," I said, "for I *do* still regard them to be different. But I know the answer! In this, the present world, there is but *one* subject: me. Where as the real world is a collective dream, a dream dreamt by many subjects . . . well, but that's not quite right, is it? Each subject is in his own world, yes, utterly. Worlds are like . . . Leibnizian monads.[5] Windowless, I suppose. Unless . . . somehow, *philosophy*, in the words themselves, connects us. But that too would depend on *which* philosophy—"

"Hold on," she said. "What did you just realize? Don't just rush on."

"That . . . *not* all philosophies are . . . equal?"

"Then let them be distinguished."

"First and foremost," I said, rushing on, "is what I would call 'the received philosophy,' the one I come programmed with. It's part of the fabric out of which self and world are constructed, part of the baggage of language. We have no choice but to accept the received philosophy up to the point where, I suppose, through the activity of philosophy itself new philosophies are generated that have not yet become viewings, actualities, *worlds*. But selves don't make philosophies; philosophies I suppose make selves as much as worlds; object and subject both equally are derivative upon philosophy . . . and yet, at the same time, there seems to be a mysterious point of contact between the subject identified in the world as a self and the subject as actualizer of the world entire . . . I don't know what else to call it but the *metaphysical* subject? God? I'm getting all confused again . . ."

She made a mock inclination. I admired her neck, the throat of a Nefertiti. Reaching into her pile of books, she withdrew a single thin volume; it was Kant's *Prolegomena to Any Future Metaphysics*. She read:

> "These my principles, because they make phenomena of the representations of the senses,

are so far from turning the truth of experience into mere illusion, that they are rather the only means of preventing the transcendental illusion, by which metaphysics has hitherto been deceived, and led to the childish endeavor of catching at bubbles, while phenomena, which are mere representations, were taken for things in themselves - an error which . . . is destroyed by the single observation, that phenomenon, as long as it is used in experience, produces truth, but the moment it transgresses the bounds of experience, and consequently becomes transcendent, produces nothing but illusion. . . . if it be really an objectionable idealism to convert actual things (not phenomena) into mere representations, by what denomination shall we distinguish that idealism which conversely makes things of mere representations? It may, I think, be called dreaming idealism, in contradistinction to the former, which may be called visionary, both of which are to be obviated by my transcendental, or, better, critical idealism."[6]

She handed the book to me and I looked at it; the work by a writer that has rightly been called "almost unreadable," (Kant himself said of his *Critique of Pure Reason* that it was "tortuously written" and "long-winded"), was a lean and succulent poem of utter illumination, speaking to me in a cadence and polyrhythm that were pure music.

"Tell me," she said, "with the philosophical lucidity you have stumbled upon within yourself in this dream, what Kant means, first, by *transcendental illusion.*"

"He means mistaking phenomena for things other than phenomena - for things in themselves."

"Then state Kant's insight using our distinction between actual and nonexistent, 'theoretical objects.' Can you?"

"Ah! The transcendental illusion, for us, would be to mistake theoretical objects for *actual* objects! To live trapped in a theory! To be . . . no, to make ourselves into nonexistent objects in an unworked and poorly conceived fiction . . . which is what the self is! That's why you call theories . . . *stories,* isn't it?"

She nodded. "Is this transcendental illusion *theoretical?* Or *actual?*"

"How do you mean?"

"Can you *point* to it?"

"Of course." I pointed: at her, at myself, at the ruins and surrounding mountains. "*We* are the illusion. The transcendental illusion *is what we are.*"

"Is that true only in these, what you call 'dream' states?"

"No! No. My God, no: in waking states it's true just as well; it's only in the imaginary dialogue of this dream that I can point to it. These present objects - my dream body, the dream sky above me and the dream earth below - everything I see in this dream appears to me to be other than what it is."

"Yes, but why do you again insert the dream clause?"

"Well, yes, I don't know why I did that—"

"Yes you do."

"You mean, because I don't *really* want to see that this applies just as much to my waking states?"

91

She nodded. "Nevertheless, let us go on, let us get to the next level. Now, what does my great lover of wisdom mean by *transcendental idealism*? Does Kant mean applying his critical technique to the 'phenomena' - what you know in your direct experience to be the objects of the present moment - so as to transcend them and attain knowledge of things in themselves existing independently of the mind, that is, actualities other than those in the present moment?"

"No."

"No? More than that: certainly not! Kant's transcendental idealism, clearly, is not a reaching outward for things in themselves as they exist independently of the mind in the 'external' world but a reaching *inward* for that which is the scaffolding of all you see, think and experience, the cause, or causes, of both the self - what Kant called the 'Phenomenal Self' - and the world - what he called the 'Phenomenal World' - in which the subject as such exists." She paused, smiling. "Kant's philosophy is a reaching by the dream from within the dream not for the fictional reality as conceived through the self but the other way, for the dreamer: the philosophical source of the existence of the world - the point of contact between subject and object, the sustaining cause of the existence of the world in space and time." She extended her hand. "Come. I will show you. We can do this."

She led me to the stone where I had first sat down after entering Delphi. She ran her hands across the dark surface and called the rock by name.

"*Omphalos*," she said. "The navel. Let us stare, together, at the navel of the world."

She lay her books and scepter atop the stone. We sat down on a smooth flat rectangular slab that might have once been part of a wall of a large building or structure.

"Touch it," she said. "Here. Put your hand on the navel of the world."

I ran my open palm against the curved stone facing us, still warm from the sun. I realized the warmth I now felt was not itself caused by the sun, since the *omphalos* stone I was touching existed only in the present moment entirely inside my mind.

"The warmth," she said, pausing for a beat, "you feel it? The smoothness? What causes that warmth you feel, the smoothness - at this instant in which you are experiencing these sensations as actualities? Is it the sun?"

"Obviously not. Nor have the winds of time worn this surface down. This surface in its every aspect, at this instant of my perceiving it, is actualized, caused to be what it at this moment is . . . I want to say by *me* - because I think I know this to be a dream, but that's not quite right, is it? Yet I reason it must nevertheless be some aspect of my own being that causes this perceived object, an idea in my mind, to have the characteristics that it right now has. For the *omphalos* I am now experiencing is not like pumice stone, nor is it like ice; it is like marbleized flesh, hard but invitingly warm and almost skinlike in its texture. So the cause of those phenomena - what I might understand reductively and theoretically in terms of *sensations* - is not the rock; I firmly believe that at this moment the rock of which this is only a dream image is not being touched by my hand, that in reality I lie inside a sleeping

93

bag inside the Oracle's chamber, with my hands *nowhere near* this rock, tucked inside a sleeping bag–"

"*Still* you believe this?"

"Yes."

"Never mind. Go on."

"So I know that the source of these perceived qualities of smoothness, warmness, resistance, and so on, are being generated by . . . well, again, I am tempted to say *myself,* but again there is the sense in which I know that *I too* am generated into this dream - into this world, I mean - just as the *omphalos* is. So the source is within . . . but that's not the right direction, since there is no actual insideness to which that predicate refers. The source of this what I am feeling within myself, this world entire, is . . . unknown, the inner unknown. I could I suppose say it is the brain that causes these objects ('internal sensations?') being now perceived by me, the subject in this dream - this world - but not only is that a very elaborate philosophy, I have no idea whatsoever how a brain - conceived as a physical (theoretical, 'subjectless) object' - *causes* actual psychological phenomena to appear as objects. No one does, as far as I know; how do chemicals (theoretical, 'subjectless objects') push these actual psychological objects which I now see (but through *philosophy* interpret as thoughts and ideas, themselves theoretical, 'subjectless objects'!) around, and how do these objects (again, interpreted philosophically as the 'objectless subjects' I call ideas and thoughts) push chemicals (theoretical 'objects') around? And I most certainly know some, but not all, of the nuances of the various philosophies and theories, I've heard lectures on the topic and read books but at this moment I can see in no uncertain terms that I am utterly and absolutely at a loss about the existence of almost everything in the world up to and including, and especially, myself." It made me laugh. "Is *this* what you want me to see?"

"I want you to keep looking," she said. "As you look ask yourself what makes experience as such possible. But keep focus on the particulars and look steadfastly at what is presently before you. What about the rock's shape?"

"It goes without saying," I said. "This shape I see presently is in no way caused by a rock 'out there' *(a nonexistent object)!* Even if I remember the shape of the rock which was once a object in my (now past) perceptions of the (then) present moment, the (then) actual (but now, at best, theoretical) object - the 'rock out there' - is not the cause of what I see here. Rather, it is some aspect of myself that is the cause. My physical eyes (theoretical, *nonexistent* objects), I firmly believe, are at this very moment closed shut (and except for in my theories I have no eyes'). No light goes from that rock - the one 'out there' in 'the (*nonexistent*) world' conceived to exist, in theory and in fiction, beyond this dream - to a brain in which, or on whose surface which, this dream is presently (in theory) occurring. Even if my brain somehow conceptually stored an image of the *omphalos* when I first entered Delphi (assuming that I did!) such that it is now using it as a sort of conceptual template to generate this perception, the present object - the perceived phenomenon of this rock-apparition I am at this moment having - is immediately caused . . . again, I want to say by *me*. But I also know it is not *me* in the sense of this perceiving subject, nor any aspect of the self. But it is, nevertheless, some aspect of my own *being* in whom *I* subsist as a imaginary - no, as an actual! - character in a dream, yet in some strange sense *am*." I touched the rock again. "And yet, at the same time, I must admit that at this moment I do not really know who *I* - this conscious subject, experiencing this world from a first person point of view, *am*. Isn't that absurd? When in the first dream I thought I was Descartes, I believed with complete certainty that I knew who I was and that I was, in reality, Descartes; now that I recall, with complete certainty, that I am not Descartes but Kolak, I come to the inexorable conclusion that I who know who I am do not know who I am! Indeed, I can make far more positive assertions about that dream rock than about this dream self as whom I presently find myself identified!"

"Listen. When you 'wake up' from this 'dream' it will be dawn. Go to the *omphalos* in your 'waking' state and mediate upon it exactly in the way we are now doing. And when you do that, in your so-called 'waking' state, I want you to remember what you've just heard yourself say in this dream, what you've heard me say. Remember, too, Plato's words, about the light. Then – and only then - ask yourself while looking at the *omphalos* what the light you see *is*. Remember: the light. Remember the light, remember . . ."

She kissed me and disappeared.

ENDNOTES

[1] I now think that all 'realizations' are, ultimately, questions, though they do not always take the form of a question

[2] In the *Blue and Brown Books*, where he says, "Thinking is not something I do, but something that happens to me." See, also, Kolak's commentary in *Wittgenstein's Tractatus*, Daniel Kolak, trans., Mayfield 1998.

[3] Plato, *The Republic*, Benjamin Jowett trans., reprinted in Daniel Kolak, *From Plato to Wittgenstein: The Historical Foundations of Mind*, Wadsworth 1994, pp. 7-8.

[4] Schopenhauer, *The World as Will and Representation*, E. F. J. Payne, trans., Dover 1966, pp. 3-6; reprinted with emendations by Daniel Kolak in *The Mayfield Anthology of Western Philosophy*, 1998.

[5] See discussions of Leibniz in Daniel Kolak, *From the Presocratics to the Present: A Personal Odyssey*, Mayfield 1998.

[6] Immanuel Kant, *Prolegomena to Any future Metaphysics*, trans. by G.J. Mahaffy, with emendations by Daniel Kolak reprinted in *The Mayfield Anthology of Western Philosophy*, 1998.

[7] Indeed, in some sense theories I think *are* eyes.

FOUR

THE

DREAM

PHILOSOPHY

It is like this: We are asleep. (I have said this once before, and it is true.) Our life is like a dream. But in our better hours we wake up just enough to realize that we are dreaming. Most of the time, though, we are fast asleep. I cannot awaken myself! I am trying hard, my dream body moves, but my real one does not stir. This, alas, is how it is!

Ludwig Wittgenstein

I AWOKE BATHED IN THE CREPUSCULAR light of dawn. A warm razor of gold slid between two pillars through the bluish misty air, settling on my face. Greek sunrise: pink rose blush clouds wafting blood red through a green crown of pines along the side of a bedeviled mountain, an erotic exorcism of night still holding tight the shadows, deep creviced pools of black ink, an embrace of ruin.

Camping takes the routine away. Nothing is easy. You go through the morning ritual, pursued by feverdreams, a desire and aching to write. I reached for my notebook . . . *the last entry was two days old!* All those pages I thought I had filled in during the middle of the night by candlelight when I had woken up from that first dream were completely blank. I had never woken up! That too was but a dream. I felt like screaming. There was nothing to do but start again:

I just woke up from a dream in which . . .

The notebook fills itself up, memories of dreams leaking out onto the bloated pages through the tip of your fountain pen.

I sit at the rock, *omphalos*, trembling in the heat, staring at the navel of the world. This is Greece. What you came for but never expected. I run my open palm against the curved stone, warm in the morning, marbleized flesh, hard but invitingly warm, skinlike.

The thought of coffee: Greek ink, bittersweet black, wishing I had some because neither the thoughts nor the awareness are forthcoming; I should have told the landlady to pack some with my lunch. I felt frightened, as empty as above me the big blue was everywhere and nowhere, endless. The dreams had drained the well and left me dry at the bottom of a bottomless pit. I had to force my thinking and my attention into a groove but it kept skipping, philosophy the way I had been taught felt strangely unnatural, an intrusion - worse, an invasion. I felt the foreigner, the proverbial stranger in the strange land made falsely familiar not by the secret lover's touch but by the brutal hands of conquest. There was something spoiled in me, utterly decrepit. A dream like that, a place like this, and I am the scared tourist with the notebook and camera bag. Decrepit.

I stood up. What was wrong? Nothing. Except for a few moments I had deceived myself into forgetting by remembering. I was thinking like a real man thinks, which is to say I was not thinking at all. Wide awake, I was barely existing. What was missing? The awareness, with me during every moment of contact with Philosophy, that the world is a dream.

As I stood there on that precipice, a real man in the real world, I felt shamed by the obviousness projecting itself through me onto the scene. Poised glee, self-discovery, the smugness of being someone, it was all a disinfecting whitewash, literally eyewash, inert, passive, horrible. This is what we call life, consciousness, identity, reality? *Real.* Suddenly I hated that word. It was less the emptiness of the concept than the way it made you so full of yourself. I understood for the first time what *vanity* meant. Occasionally we allow ourselves the realization that the world is a dream, just as occasionally in a lucid dream we allow our selves to realize that we are dreaming. In most dream and waking states *I,* the subject, live in an utterly unenlightened state. I see the objects in my consciousness as things in themselves. I cannot help but do so, since as Kant taught us (and Philosophy had finally helped me to see) this is a necessary condition for the having of experience. The unenlightened, and what Hegel called 'unhappy,' consciousness¹ is not an evolutionary step in the historical development of the world toward self-realization through self-consciousness, as Hegel would have liked to imagine, nor the awakening of the slumbering pantheistic solipsistic God, as Spinoza would have most passionately conceived. (Suddenly having lost my eyes it seemed I had grown new eyes with which to see what I had never before been able: the *visions* of the philosophers.) No; the stupidity of living in the dark is itself a necessary condition for the presence of light, the existence of consciousness, the philosophical illumination of the world.

So then what was the problem? I will use myself as an example (for there is no other). In my dream I saw objects as I now did - not as parts of myself, as complementary to the subject, but as if they were *things*. Yet in the dream I understood through the guiding presence of Philosophy that the dream was a dream and it utterly humbled, enthused and disturbed me! This was not the pious humility of, say, a religious awakening to God, a being greater than one's self. If anything, it was just the opposite. Instead of humbling oneself before some greater other, some superior otherness, it was an opening up to oneself, seeing that there is more to one's own being than can be conceived in any theory or understood by any philosophy, resulting not in the comforting faith of religious self-deception but the disconcerting doubt of ultimate philosophical self-actualization. Except now, in the 'real world,' awake, I was instead in a gross and exaggerated state of mock enlightenment, where I couldn't wait but write down the vainglorious truth that everything is a dream, my dream, that whether dreaming or awake I am in a dream! I was as bad as any religious zealot, worse, for there was in me not even the pretense of humility. This I think is why Socrates tried to teach us not to write philosophy down, so as to exorcise the dogmatic faith of the religious and scientific converts who deep down feel it is all a clever conjuring trick and don't for a moment feel any of it because even in their dumb cleverness they are far too intelligent, too brilliant, too professional to be transformed.

Truth is, I knew I was both in my dream and waking state in contact only with myself and then with the world – regardless of whether any 'world' existed independently of my mind. I knew there was no other way for it to be! Eyes are never windows, they can't be. Yet something in me snuffs this truth into a dogmatic exegesis too clever and scientific by half, which itself is part of some inner conspiracy from within to usurp the higher into the lower, the lower being the self. In the 'real' world I dream that I'm not dreaming. In the 'dream' I dream that I am dreaming. Yet the latter – in those strangest and most unrealizable dream states of consciousness which have been described as 'states of madness' – brings me closer to the truth than do my most sober waking states. At the root of the problem was the issue of control, whether the world and I in our most ultimate state are in control or whether it all is flux, chaos, some unimaginable, incomprehensible Heraclitan maelstrom of opposites . . .

I thus realized with growing discomfort that these were not the same world at all: I had subtly in the back of my mind - as I'm sure you do from one world to the next - hidden from myself the borders between the worlds in which I exist, the discontinuous identity which Philosophy had tried to get me to comprehend. The 'dream' world in which Philosophy and I had carried out our disturbing dialogue and the 'real' world in which I now found myself in a monologue (that even in its most outlandish narrative was deeply comforting), were not the same world; they lived in different philosophies: the dream philosophy and the real philosophy. The *real* philosophy says I am in the world and there are others in the world with me but the world is not in me nor in them. The *dream* philosophy says I am in the world and the world is in me and there is no other. It was as if I had two philosophies, one 'true' and one 'false,' by which I lived two very different sorts of lives; lives with and for others vs. lives with and for myself. Encountering the dream philosophy within myself allowed me to see that the former was a lesser form of existence than the latter, that in our waking lives we have it assbackwards and don't know it, that everything - everything - hinged on the dubious distinction between self and other.

A moment earlier I would have gladly ripped off my clothes and danced a pagan dance to get Philosophy, and the dream, back; fortunately, I didn't have to: with a gentle pine-scented breeze descending in rolling waves down Mt. Parnassus, in a sudden flash of insight I realized everything was exactly as in the dream. Reality had suddenly and invisibly removed itself like a veil and my world returned itself to me. This is not my body, that is not omphalos, none of this is other than what was before me in the dream: ideas, objects perceived in the mind through the subject, ignited into present (and necessarily perspectival!) actuality by the light of consciousness. I was now, as in the dream, the subject

103

identified as a self; my body was an idea, a dream body, and in that quiet moment of passivity I saw and experienced in all its glory the durationless dream philosophy of the present moment in which - be it dream or waking state - the light of consciousness ignites me and my world into existence.

The actual world - this world presently in front of me - and everything in it, including the perceiving subject - *I*, me, the self – is my world. Be it dream or waking state, the only world in which *I* will ever find myself - speaking now not of some 'theoretical world' describable in words or recalled in memory or imagined in theory but a world perceived in space and time – is a centered world, a world at whose center am I. The world I am in is a world with a view and I am the viewer and the viewed whether I know it or not. I, a conscious being, this perceiving subject, am located at the center of my world essentially bound in space and time, identified in the present moment, here and now, in this actual (not theoretical!) body in space without a head and this actual (not theoretical!) mind in time. The body and mind in my experience exist not as descriptions in some timeless, abstract theory, but in actual space and time by which I mean not the abstract, mathematical space and time (of four dimensions? Of eleven dimensions?), but the space and time perceived in actual experience. And why weren't these just so many words to me? Because in that moment when everything is righted by philosophy the theoretical becomes actual and you can see it, know it, be in the mask and enjoy it for no one but yourself. Which is just to say, in that moment but only for that moment, you don't so much find your self as self-actualize, and die.

The world breathes in. The world breathes out. You die and go on living. The self is the mask of consciousness. The subject is the life breath of the world.

The only concrete way I have of explaining this supra-conscious moment of self-actualization is to liken it to the subtle and tremendous difference between a book written as a first-person narrative in the passive voice and a book written in a first-person narrative but in an active voice. Both texts have a point of view. Both are written in the first person. Descartes was as far as I know the first philosopher to present philosophy like that, in the first person and in the active voice and until that moment I had never fully understood why. It's a subtle difference and only a make-believe analogy but it is what makes the difference between living on automatic pilot, knowing just about everything, and wondering just about nothing, and living without any authority, knowing just about nothing, and wondering just about everything. It literally makes all the difference in the world.

Another strange discovery! The mind that understands mind as mind is a mind self-actualized. Self-actualized is the mind that does not by attachment to the self hold on to itself – its thoughts, beliefs and ideas - but a mind that breathes, illuminated and unattached to its ideas, and does not even pretend to have found itself or to stand still. In that moment you are for that moment at an interface, a fulcrum between worlds in which anything is possible, in which the text swallows itself. You lose your self. Time stops. Alternate philosophies avail themselves with which to view everything, even your own viewing. In the moment but only for that moment I, the subject in my world, am not passive to myself nor to my world but selfless, alive. And death? In so far as these objects presently before me are perspectival objects in space (i.e., a perspectival space, that is, a space with a vanishing point and I am both that vanishing point and point of appearance!) they cease to exist as objects when they are no longer thus perceived. Berkeley was right. Oh, how Berkeley, that poor, misunderstood and much abused philosophical genius, was right! This world you presently find yourself in will literally vanish the moment you cease to view it, as surely and exactly as all dreams vanish without the dreamer. For each and every aspect of the world known to you at this moment as *the* world, your one and only, in truth requires your presence, the presence of the subject: the subject is the sun of the universe within, the light of consciousness. And the aspect of you that vanishes with the objects – what the subject is identified as in the dream – is your on again, off again, self. Don't remember a word of this, forget it and look at your thoughts, perceptions, feelings - *look, don't think* I can hear Philosophy reminding me - and you will see how exhilarating it is to lose yourself and in that selfless yet utterly selfish purely subjective moment find yourself and the world both standing at the very same spot, vanishing and appearing both at once. That spot is *you.*

How long does a world last? According to quantum physics, the world is between fifteen and twenty billion years old. That's far too old. According to Christian theology, the world is about five thousand years old. That's far more accurate, but still too optimistic and nowhere near the true mark. According to Gautama Buddha, the world is always new, only a few seconds old. That is more accurate than the scientific or Christian estimate but a bit too pessimistic. The correct age of the world, as far as I can tell, was best guessed at by Bertrand Russell. (It's satisfying, I think, to know that it took a philosopher like Russell to get closest to the truth but only when he did not mean to). The correct age of the world is about five minutes, exactly as Russell once supposed - the length of most dreams.[2]

The thought made me laugh out loud. The laughter echoed from the mountain, back and forth, across the ruins.

The subject is unbound by its worlds as it is unconnected by its memories. Experience disappears (within at least every five minutes or so) 'into the past' along with all the objects of perception. After all, I reminded myself, was it not I in that dream who was Descartes? What did I know of myself then, in *that* world? Before I left for Greece my girlfriend had told me she had dreamt she had gone on a job requiring her to kill somebody (she couldn't remember, after she 'awoke,' who and in the dream it didn't seem to matter). She went on the job, she killed this person, but her 'backup' - a driver who was supposed to be picking her up - was late and she was very angry with him. When my girlfriend, who in 'real life' believes she is not a killer for the mob but a reporter, asked me about her dream, she noted how absurdly funny it is that in a dream we just accept everything and go along with anything, even when we are completely 'out of character,' and what did I as a student of philosophy think about that? But that's precisely it: you think you are you and have always been, that your history is continuously what it seems, that you are this very persona or personality to whom you are wedded at the moment in what you call your waking world and then in your dream you can be somebody else entirely. You assume without thinking - it is invisibly written into the invisible theory - that it is all one and the same world but in the meta-theory that is writing itself here, it isn't. Each five minute time and space (it's actually is quite a large manifold, in terms of miles[3]) is utterly disjoint from all the others (and here I might as well tell you we cannot parenthetically say, 'except in theory,' for there is no theory that works to connect even mind to world, much less mind to mind to world). What makes it seem otherwise is you: the presence of the subject identified as the self, the perceiving subject in your world, usually known to itself only in a passive state. But you can be awakened into actuality - self-actualized - by the dream philosophy: lose your head and lose yourself, find yourself selfless. (Don't rejoice. Death is at the border.)

Without a perceiving subject there are no objects: no *I*, no world. What there is without you is not a world but a virtually subsisting realm of abstract modality consisting possibly of numbers, sets, theories, programs, and probably a boundless array of logical beings whose abstract nature is such that they need never be created to exist, at least not in the subsistent, virtual realm of infinite possibility transcendent of space, time and consciousness. Mind, the realm of actuality, consists in space and time beyond which, or without which, in the abstract realm there is no present moment, no actuality, no *inside*. Unlike actual dream worlds constituted as such in consciousness, the perceiving subject whose presence ignites objects into actuality, being as conceived in the abstract sense does not exist as a world because it cannot exist. (This of course leaves ample room for nonexistent objects, nonexistent subjects, and nonexistent worlds.)

To be is not to be. I am not what I am. The endpoints of real philosophy are but the starting points of dream philosophy. Or, less simply: dreaming or awake, I am always dreaming. Dreams ignite my world into existence. I am a windowless monad existing in a dream philosophy beyond the theoretical space of real philosophy (which is a mathematical, not actual, space - think algebraic fields) dreaming with theoretical eyes closed, dreaming with nonexistent eyes open, always dreaming.

Lacking the presence of an embodied Philosophy, reason suddenly rushed to close the door of my raving speculations. All right, I said to myself as I sat down on what looked exactly like the slab in the dream (and how did I know that?), let me think about this as an irresponsible student should. I faced the *omphalos* stone. I am that object's subject; for even if someone else were with me at the ruins of Delphi, looking at the *omphalos* stone, that mind would be attending in its own world not to this very object presently actualized in my mind as seen from this unique perspectival vanishing point, but a rather similar perceptual ('subjective) object' whose subject would be not me, but him (or her). Actual existence requires subjectivity: this actual object *is* my object, solely so. This seemed relatively clear. I went on looking at the stone.

Except for the daytones, the *omphalos* stone as an object presently before me (i.e., the perceived and therefore

109

perspectival, that is, the "subjective object," constituted in qualities essentially requiring a "seeing from somewhere") - looked exactly like the one in my dream. But now I wondered: how can you tell whether an object (think, "subjective object") in the present moment looks similar to some 'real' object (think, "theoretical ('subjectless) object'") recalled from the past? It's not as if I, the perceiving subject, have some sort of double vision, wherein I compare the object now with the earlier (no longer present) object, so as to be able to tell they look similar. There is just the object now in the present moment: actuality requires subjectivity and subjectivity is essentially perspectival, that is, spatiotemporal. Thus all I ever have before me is apperception.[4] This philosophical apperception comes with what Bertrand Russell called (did anyone listen?) the seeming "sense of familiarity." In saying this I merely mean that this "seeming familiarity" is actualized in the object itself. That this seeming familiarity was something my mind added to the objects I was now, in my 'waking state,' seeing, was not a rational deduction, nor any sort of intellectual inference that the stone now looks like the stone in my dream. The stone just was in its very presence "familiar," immediately so, without my having to (or even being able to) compare this present actuality with any other. And this was just as true of the actual *omphalos* stone presently before me, perceived in that 'waking state,' as it was of my recalled (theoretical) 'perception' from the day before when I first arrived at Delphi.

In other words, it made little difference whether I was trying to compare a dream state with a waking state, or trying to compare two waking states; the conscious "act" of recognition (in the sense of *act* meant by Fichte and also Husserl[5]) - "I've seen this thing before, it looks familiar," etc. - is not a conscious *act* at all, it is a passively (and covertly) received quality along with the rest of the object, like the thoughts themselves emerging as if out of the void. And the void (and what is that - non-perspectival, non-subjective, unimaginable existence?) is of course as nonexistent as 'reality' (but perhaps less philosophically implausible; Kant comes to mind).

The proof of this aspect of the dream philosophy is laughably simple, once you realize it. You know by your own understanding that in dreams you are surrounded by all manner of objects that have come into existence in that moment of perception. Yet you are not startled, you do not scream, you simply accept each item as if it were a permanent, fixed reality known by you as such. For instance, you dream yourself among the ruins: walls, stones, temples pop into existence, literally, from nothing, actualized at that moment of perception. Yet you 'recognize' them, accept them as ancient. But in dreams even the most ancient ruins are brand new; as, also, are *you*. Why then don't you scream? Why are you not screaming now? (And why am I not?)

I realized, too, that what was true of objects like the stone in front of me was also true of me, the subject. With a slight feeling of queasy terror - not unlike the earlier sensation of my world turning upside down, except nothing happens - I realized that I-now, this 'awake dream' self, 'felt' similar to previous states of consciousness actualized at other times but

111

that not only had I absolutely no way of checking whether this was so in actuality, I always felt to myself familiar! There I had been Descartes in the dream and I recognized everything about myself with the same utter and intimate familiarity that I now did. Except I now 'recognized' *this* self as the 'true' self and *that* self as the 'false' self. This 'recognition,' which comes out of the actual experience of the instant, inscribes (imbibes?) itself into whatever is presented to the subject - literally, making each new event of existence fit into a recognizable schema – and spreads outward from me onto the objects themselves. The subject is thus the actualizer of its world - inclusive of all the objects in perception - in virtue of this strange, noncognitive process of identification by which something that has existed but for a few moments - such as each and every one of the objects presently before you - appears as fixed, permanent, as having an age, a history, of having been around for more than five minutes. Consciousness is the metaphysical glue, the confabulatory element that makes the world concrete. (Are you howling yet?)

I thus saw what I had never realized about the problem of personal identity: it wasn't just that I have no way of establishing, in experience, that I, a self at one time am numerically identical to some (presently non-actual) self at some previous time. Nor is the problem that I have no way even of establishing, in experience, whether these selves, located as they are in distinct (nonconcurrent) worlds, are similar. The problem is that everything is in each world brand new. Both individuated object and identified subject come into existence as actualities in the *now* (Dedekind comes to mind) and then in a matter of seconds or minutes they are gone. So it is worse than merely the epistemological problem of how I recognize myself "over time," given that any state of "recognition" occurs, essentially and necessarily, at a time. It is the ontological problem of getting from there to here, into this world that has never before this moment existed and, as such, will never exist again. The fact is that one's own presence as the subject in the world just feels familiar in the instant of existence, along with whatever memories present themselves, whether in dream or waking states of consciousness that come always with their own sense of familiarity, of obviousness, imbibed into them - just like the rock I see, the *omphalos* stone, the navel.

Staring at that rock, I realized that I, the perceiving subject, was in that present moment objectified into a mind and body as a numerically identical being over time even though the objects in which I existed as a self could not possibly be the vehicles of any such identity. That is, as Berkeley as well as Hume clearly saw and recognized in their philosophy, states of consciousness - be they "dream" or "waking" states - come and go and do not persist with identity over time. So whence then, I wondered, this all-pervasive sense of one's own identity? I don't mean just the sense of being some particular person, heightened as it is through attachment to the self, but very closely related: the feeling of being someone, anyone, at all, which is best apprehended in a state of selflessness. And it is this selfless self-identification as part of the self-actualization process that makes it possible for

113

me, the subject, to exist, with identity, identified in one world as one self (Descartes) and identified in another world as another (Kolak). Again, the fact is that there is no *epistemological* basis for such recognition – the sensation of identity is not, itself a cognition of any sort. It is more like a feeling, an emotion that no rationalization process can dispel or touch. (Was this the sort of thing Wittgenstein said philosophers must never talk about, which had tried to express itself in the silence of the dream?[6])

In other words, just like you, I felt as if I were the same being over time; how did I know? I didn't. One moment I thought I knew who I was because I thought I was Descartes. In another moment I think I know who I am because I know I am not Descartes but Kolak. You right now as you read these words no doubt think you are you, the perceiving subject in relation to your present objects, in virtue of being Mr. Suchandsuch or Ms. Soandso, a name you don't so much learn to go by as accept in the same way in the dream I accepted 'Descartes' and now accepted 'Kolak:' as if you are one and the same self over time, identical to yourself over time in virtue of some sort of continuity! But such continuity there is only in theory, not in actual experience, sustained through identification as a self.

Clearly, the content of any state of consciousness, as such, is not identical to any other. The state of perceiving an apple is not the state of perceiving an orange. What about the state of consciousness itself - not the object perceived but the perceiving subject? Consciousness, I suddenly realized, is not a psychological or physiological (abstract, theoretical) but

114

metapsychological, metaphysiological (actual, spatiotemporal) state of mind - what I would venture to call a *philosophical state of mind.* By this I merely mean: no theory *touches* conscious experience.

What, then, are the identity conditions for conscious states understood as philosophical states of mind? Interestingly enough, I realized that I, the subject identified as this very self, do not even know what those identity conditions are! Second, assuming that there were such identity conditions, or even that I could construct them, the lesser bond of similarity between states of consciousness is itself impossible to ascertain in experience. I thought once more of Buddha and Hume and wished I could talk again to Philosophy about my present perplexity experienced not through reading Buddha or Hume or Kant but by staring at a rock and communing with myself. It made me laugh again. Did one need Greece for this, I wondered, or Buddha, or Hume? I wanted suddenly to run to my notebooks again, so as not to forget this - as if mere words in a notebook, bloated little inkblots, could contain philosophy, or evoke it, or relate to the world in any way by the sacrificial spill of their black blood! And yet, recalling what little I knew of semiotics[7], in a strange and mysterious way, the words not only related both to the subject and the object, at the moment they seemed to be the only bridge. As if language itself was the virtual wire bridging not only subject to world but subject to subject, *I* to *I.* The subject and everything that went along with it, from thought to language to the self, had a necessary function in the grand scheme of things! If I didn't believe this I would not be writing now. Either that, or I am even more conceited or self-deceived (they amount to the same thing) than I think I am.

I felt suddenly inextricably, inexplicably happy, except in a completely new and detached way. Perhaps I sensed that the insights from my 'dream states' had survived into my 'waking states.' I realized, with sudden shock, so nebulous yet electric: mulling over my identity, perplexed as to whether I even had one, I had been overjoyed by the sense that some karmic thing does indeed 'survive' across the uncrossable threshold between worlds, as if this philosophical self-actualization itself mattered more than identity. As if existence was not a thing in any sense of the word, nor an object nor even the (passive) self but the momentary presence of self-actualization. And what is that? A philosophical (*not* psychological, for it is in the unknown) sense of connection to one's self and to one's world, of some exotically vivacious philosophical profundity coursing through your veins like a river running through the world connecting everything, so tumultuous it didn't matter who you were so long as this life force, this perhaps Bergsonian *élan vital*, is there.[8] Illusion? Great art is illusion, a great and grand illusion, but it too can make you feel this way.[9] Except *feel* is not the right word, that is too psychological; *be* is the better word. One imagines Homer, Parmenides, Shakespeare, DaVinci, Mozart, *being* that way. Bunuel: art is a razor to the eye. Kafka: a book is an axe at the frozen sea within us. Philosophy, the world, and the philosophical self-actualization of *I am:* the unholy trinity.

Suddenly anything and everything seemed possible because in that moment I, the world, and philosophy seemed absolutely impossible! Poetry? Let there be poetry, and music, philosophy and science too. I wanted all at once everything, to know everything, to experience and be everything and everyone.

Omphalos. Kneeling before a rock I am at the navel of the world, I am at the temple at Delphi, I am in Greece, I am in rapture.

I spent much of the rest of the morning sitting on that rock, in the thin shade of a young pine. I ate my *kourabiedes*, conical buttercakes coated with icing sugar, drank mineral water spiced with the famous lemon ouzo indigenous to the region, and made no notes. Sometimes raising the bottle to my lips I would say,

"Eis 'ygeia sas, René."

Or, just, "*Sygeia.*"

I fought with black flies. Occasionally I would walk into the sunlight at the edge of the colonnade, stretch, return to the *omphalos* stone. My thoughts were refreshingly still, perspicuous in their simplicity and intensity; not that I didn't have them but that they weren't, as it were, going anywhere. They were just there, like me, like that ancient rock, like the surrounding ruins. I teetered between being no one, everyone, and just myself but not caring one way or the other, the moment was in itself already all that and more. Nothing seemed to be going anywhere, though there was a feeling of intense chaos pressing everything forth into instantaneous, durationless, eternal actuality. It was like being at the center of a hurricane. I felt centered, as if consciousness had clefted

117

itself into a smile that could not be seen but only felt. How appropriate, to be centered, here, alone, smiling at the center of the world.

In the afternoon an old man astride a donkey came down the cliff. He was from the nearby modern village of Phocis. His name was Hermes, which even when I had first met him didn't make me smile; here the most common names are Aristotle, Socrates, Aphrodite. Aphrodite works in the coffee shop, she makes up your bed, she gives out traffic tickets. Aristotle is a boy who stole your good walking sandals that you left outside the door, an old man who fixed your backpack, a bus driver. Socrates is a waiter in the greasy 'inauthentic' Greek restaurant you swore never to step foot in again.

But now, as I shared a tumbler of *retsina* with him in silence, I smiled uneasily at my - what shall I call it? - snobbishness? False expectations? Urbanized stupidity? You think of Plato and Socrates seicheing in their milky white robes, ghostlike holy figures with Oxford accents. You conveniently ignore Socrates' apology in the Apology for being such a peasant, such an ineloquent speaker, begging his illustrious and learned audience to not think him crude and dumb for his manner, that they should listen before they sentence him to death for corrupting the youth which he did of course and so they did anyway. You forget their togas were multicolored robes, each groove of the grand white pillars a different color, the statues painted, even the eyes, all utterly pastiche.

The worst insult you can throw at someone in this part of

the world is to call him a peasant. Hermes, however, was in point of fact a peasant. I had paid him some trifling to bring me food, which he did. As I tried but failed to chat with him he fingered his *koumbologi*, amber patience beads. He had a bad eye, a sinister pallor, and swarthy, sunburned leather skin.

Hermes had never asked me what an American college student was doing in Greece out of season spending days and nights among the ruins. He only cared that I would pay him, in advance, the amount he requested. During what they here simply call 'the war,' he had been an *andarte*, a resistance fighter, as I had found out from Aphrodite the landlady who seemed not to like him very much.

The bread was good and fresh. The goat cheese was still cool because he had wrapped it well and packed it carefully inside the drink and fruit.

"What's this?"

It was a thermos full of Turkish coffee.

"Aphrodite sends it."

"Tell her thanks." I had forgotten to mention coffee. I sniffed at the still warm fish cooked in white wine and garlic, the green-pepper and onion salad with eggs, then closed the packet up.

"Where are the olives?"

He reached into his rucksack and pulled out a half empty jar of fat blue-black Amphissa olives.

"I can give you money back."

"You can bring more olives tomorrow. What is the weather?"

"How do I know?"

119

"You don't hear what the weather will be?"

"No."

He pocketed his tip without looking. His donkey stared straight at me with glazed eyes, tail swatting at the black flies. Hermes took the reins.

"So long," he said.

"Ever been to the ruins?"

"Sure. I pass by. Many times."

"What do you think of them?"

"Hm?" Sighing, he stood there holding the reins, unmoving, visibly bothered by my still trying to engage him in conversation.

"You know their significance?"

"I do not give them the significance of the *touristes*." He intended it as an insult. I wondered why he didn't just walk away. But he didn't.

"Is there anything you can tell me about them?"

"No."

"Anything at all."

"No." Now he suddenly laughed, a deep-throated belly laugh.

"You are in a hurry?"

"I have no family."

"Never married?"

"Killed in the war."

"No wife?"

"Killed in the war."

"Never remarried?"

"One wife was enough." He laughed again.

"No children?"

He shrugged, oddly, with just one shoulder; perhaps a wound. "Two. Killed. They were killed. They killed them."

"I'm sorry, I . . . I'm sorry."

He shrugged, again, with the one shoulder. Again I expected he would go now. Instead, he started talking. "We used to live up there beyond those cliffs, on that plateau. See? No, look! There." He turned and pointed with his eyes.

"What do you know about it?"

"We used to call it *Locorea*."

"What's there now?"

"Nothing. The Corycian cave. You can go up there and have a look at that. When it is hot outside in there it is cool and pleasant."

"Anything else?"

He shrugged again, the one shoulder. "We moved down here for the adjoining farmlands."

"When?"

"Five thousand years ago."

"Who?"

"We, the people."

"Oh."

"We called it *Pytho*, not Delphi. Our oracle belonged to the Earth Goddess. It was guarded by the serpent-God Python. Apollo slew him and impregnated the Goddess," he chuckled, "and the oracle became ours. That's how Greece was born."

We didn't say anything for a few moments.

"Her ruins don't interest you?"

He shrugged again. "Ever lose anyone?"

When I didn't answer he looked at me, cold and hard, to hide what he was thinking about. But he was thinking about his wife, his children.·

"To you these are her ruins," he said, his eyes welling up in a way that embarrassed me. "You think we are stupid because we avoid them, that we don't understand their significance. These are not her ruins. Not *hers.* Ours."

He swallowed hard and wiped the sweat from his brow with the back of his hand. He turned and quickly started back up the hill, suddenly a very weak and tired old man in a hurry, uneasy on his feet, sifting his prayer beads with one hand, pulling the donkey with the other.

"So long. Hermes."

The rasp of cicadas in the surrounding pines swelled and fell as the sun hammered down the mountain. I ate my meal in the shade of the solitary remaining wall of a treasury building from which during Roman times Nero is said to have pillaged 500 statues. Everything was excellent except the wine, which had a taste of resin, as if the vineyard had been along a pine forest. It wasn't as bad, though, as its turpentine aftertaste which even the delicious honey-and-curd flan did not fix. In the windless, early afternoon sun the wine gave me a slight headache for which I was mighty glad to have Aphrodite's coffee.

Afterwards I had a swim at the Castalian spring that flowed from a cleft between the rocks near the sanctuary. When I saw a group of tourists approaching down the winding road from Phocis I went up into the pines and spent the afternoon filling another notebook. Later a cool breeze blew up across the valley from the Plistus river as I dozed in the soft shadows of the pines. It was a dreamless sleep, as if all the dream stuff had been used up (a stupid thought), as if energy was being held in reserve for what was yet to come (that I can believe).

In the late afternoon, after the tourists left I walked the ruins. (They were Italian students, I heard the singsong cadence of voices drifting up in the breeze, a hilarious rendition of a well-known song whose words they must have memorized without any meaning, for it came out with a possessive added: "Let's my people go-o, let's my people go.") Using the maps of a travel book written in the 2nd century A.D. by Pausanias (far more accurately detailed than the 'current' one printed by the tourist office), I found the three empty holes that once held the tripod support of intertwined serpents stolen by Constantine 'the Great' after the battle of Plataea (479 BC), a treasure I had seen in the Hippodrome in Istanbul. It cost the lives of 10,000 men and the sacking of six villages each containing roughly 1,000 women and children to make those three holes in that stone. That's just over three thousand men and two thousand women and children per hole.

The main sanctuary is a large, walled rectangle; I measured it to see for myself that it was indeed, like the Parthenon at the Acropolis, a "golden rectangle," based upon the proportion known and worshipped by the Pythagoreans as the "golden ratio," called "the divine proportion" by Kepler and considered insignificant by most philosophers and mathematicians today. This ratio forms a series of patterned numbers called a fibonacci series (after Leonardo Fibonacci, alias "Leonardo of Pisa," b. 1175 A.D.). It shows up in the helix structure of plants such as *Achillea ptarmica*, popularly known as sneezewort, the breeding patterns of rabbits, the spiral structures of galaxies, sunflowers, and the energy quanta states of electrons - not to mention its representation in the genealogy of drone bees, which are all over the place here. Oh, and the equiangular spirals found *on diminutive foraminifera* shells, which you can only see through a microscope, and mollusk shells, up to the large chambered nautilus shell that you can find strewn all along the beaches here. All are patterned on numbers based on the golden ratio. And of course what no travel, mathematics, or philosophy book points out is that there also just happen to be more than a few sunflowers growing on these slopes and tons of sneezewort plants all around the ruins of the sanctuary, and that as the late afternoon sun ripens the drone bees seem to flock to them. So you lie back, sip your coffee, and wait for the galaxies to come out.

I must have fallen asleep for I awoke with a start, on my back, spread-eagled on that rock, my eyes smarting from having fallen asleep facing the sun. Penumbral shadows reddened the entire place. My skin felt parched from the dry, windless heat. The cicadas were a maddening swirl of hypnotic tempos. I rubbed my eyes. My first thought was that Hermes had drugged me. The light seemed to have burned itself through the lids, overexciting the phosphenes, so that even closed it was all white hot. When I opened my eyes still they would not adjust; the afternoon glow was everywhere, in everything, absorbed into the stones as heat. The only motion in the wedded stillness were the emerald lizards scurrying like living bracelets across the hallowed rocks.

In this heightened state of luminous drunkenness thought descended with the sun into the horizon like the thick thirst-quenching rain clouds gathering along the top of Mt. Parnassus coalescing as if out of nowhere, slowly darkening the scene before my eyes. It wasn't that I had earlier, upon waking from my dream, forgotten Philosophy's words. Rather, it was that in consciously remembering them I had forgotten what they meant. Now, in the actuality of the new present moment, wide awake as the sun hovered at the horizon and the stars began to appear in the dying violet redness, I asked myself: what is this light that you are now seeing?

The scientific story: It takes a photon of light 200,000 years to reach the surface of the sun from its center where it is born in gravitational collapse, the proton-proton fusion interaction in which two atoms of hydrogen fuse into one helium atom. Then, traveling at 186,284 miles per second across the roughly 84,000,000 miles from the surface of the sun to the Earth, it takes the photon 7.5 minutes to reach the Earth; it strikes the *omphalos* stone and then in .000000001 seconds - one billionth of a second - it reflects off the carved *phaedriade* ("shining rock!") up there on those jutting cliffs and strikes the back of my eye. The light stops *here*. The photon goes no further; its little bit of energy - about a trillionth of an ampere - gets somehow translated by the incredibly sensitive rods and cones at the back of the retina into a firing rate, a number (Pythagoras comes to mind). Because of the inverse law of wavelength and mass-energy - $E = 1/\gamma$, where γ is the wavelength and E is the energy - the smaller the wavelength, the greater the energy. (Hence x-rays and microwaves, for instance, are much more lethal energy levels for humans than is visible light, while radio waves, which are of much longer wavelengths, are harmless.) And this is all somehow encoded and recognized by the light-sensitive part of the human organism, consisting of the eye, the optic "nerve," and brain centers responsible for processing the numbers associated with vision (most notably, the calcarine fissure, the site within the brain most active in perception - in theory, of course, I heard Philosophy's voice within me say).

What I just described are not actual objects as Philosophy defined them but, rather, "theoretical ('subjectless, nonexistent) objects.'" Yet everything just described - from the photon to the optic nerve, from the sun to the brain - is reducible in current physical theory to constellations of quantum particles which themselves (in theory) 'exist' (even the physicist here must use quotes) in a superposition of states until a measurement or act of observation collapses the superposition state, understood as a wave of probability, into a wave of 'actuality.' Now, one of the "mind-boggling" aspects of the leading and most promising interpretations of quantum mechanics is that the ultimate physical constituents of reality exist in a non-actual, 'virtual' state that becomes actualized only as state-bound events in the act of measurement or

126

observation. Virtuality in physics extends the concept of an object beyond actuality into the realm of possibility, where prior to actualization each quantum particle exists (or, more accurately, subsists) in a ghostly superposition of possible states (themselves reducible, according to contemporary physicists such as John Archibald Wheeler and Stephen Hawking, to logical or mathematical 'truths,' which of course need not be created in order to exist in their Platonic state). What I was now suddenly realizing is that all the aforementioned "physical ('subjectless) objects'" that were part of the "scientific" story of perception were construed upon a false and deeply misleading dichotomy, in twentieth century physics, between the microscopic quantum world and the macroscopic world of human experience.[10] It was partly the fault of physics for following Newton rather than Descartes and Leibniz. There was no such distinction between the microscopic and macroscopic worlds. Macroscopic objects as well - the *omphalos* stone, the temple of Delphi, my body, etc. - exist as 'virtual' states of possibility until they are actualized by the light of consciousness as subjective states of the subject identified as the conscious self. The stone before me did not exist as an object extended in time because objects, as such, exist only within the actuality of the present moment, beyond which they recede out of the brief realm of actual existence back into the virtual state of mere theoretical (i.e., 'virtual') existence, mere possibility. Indeed, I mused to myself that in going from future to present to past, these very objects of which (and sequentially in which) the world entire supposedly consisted go from theoretically possible to actual to virtually

127

impossible states of affairs. For when an event lies in the future it subsists only in the virtuality of the future, as a possible actuality; once it becomes present it exists in the actuality of the present moment; once it is past it recedes into the virtuality of the past, receding from the state of actuality to possibility.

On and on I went through such thinking procedures almost mechanically, of which I am leaving out various details having to do with the physiology of perception, neurophysiological theories of brain functioning, neural network models of perception construction, connectionist and representationalist theories of mind, and so on. The point is that the current state of the art of science suggested Philosophy had been right in her subversive guidance; for the sun conceived as an object extended both in physical space and time was neither an ('actual') object and nor was it the cause of vision. Nor were the other seen (actual) objects - the rocks, the ruins, the trees, mountain and sky - the cause of vision. Rather, it was - again, as in the dream, I was tempted to say *I* - some aspect of my own being, or the being of which I was a part, that was the cause: all these things were constituted, literally, in and through my presence. That tiny photon, accessible only by theory (and perhaps, as the great 19th century physicist Ernst Mach believed, existing only in theory[11]), by itself has no direct bearing on the actual scene 'before my eyes' for the simple reason that everything I was seeing, even now when awake, was most certainly not the scene "before" my eyes but the scene after my eyes. *Physical light waves are not bright, they are dark as dark can be.* Light is the mind, it is consciousness itself. To say such things in the safety of proper philosophical context is to speak as a not easily understood pedant; to experience them here, under such an open sky, at Philosophy's temple, was to inquire not into technical felicities having to do with the nuances of semantics but to be in awe of the existence of the world and one's self in it, to allow yourself to be ravaged by the visceral angst of uncut and not easily understood raw experience, to let consciousness live and die by the actuality of the present moment.

I think I finally understood, in that moment, what Wittgenstein meant by his cryptic phrase in the *Tractatus* that "It is not how things are in the world that is mystical, but that it exists." It is the actuality of these illuminated objects, present to the mind, that is truly mystical, utterly, utterly so. One was glad at such moments to have the toiling laborers in their labyrinthine caves, the explainers, the technicians in their laboratories, the wordsmiths, the theoreticians, for they - like the elaborate, intricate, preciously fragile tools they fashion - are worth their weight in gold; but one was also glad in that perspicuous moment to not be one of them, to be as careless with one's thoughts as a bird in free flight is with wings wide-open. In such moments there is nothing elaborate, nothing intricate, nothing precious, nothing fragile about existence. The ideas soar of their own volition, hanging effortlessly in open space like metaphysical paintings painted without brushes or canvas, brilliant as diamonds and impenetrable in their momentary splendor: ideas revealed as wisdom's living monuments, inscrutable and timeless as ruins. Words, in all their argumentative arrangements, are but a tithe.

My hand upon the rock, outstretched fingers creviced in the red heat. With apologies to G.E. Moore: *This is not my hand.* With apologies to all the poor, misguided materialists in their make-believe worlds: *This is not a rock. When I "cross my eyes," the hand I see splits like an amoeba, the surface of the rock divides.* Physical objects, as traditionally conceived in physical theory, do not divide in response to states of consciousness (nor, in state of the art quantum theory, are they three dimensional). Microscopic, quantum physical objects, on the other hand, and mental objects as ordinarily conceived in theories of perception, can and do so respond to the mind; indeed, according to the "many worlds" interpretation of quantum mechanics, the entire physical universe divides itself every time an observer makes a measurement.[12] Or, to be as crude as I like: I shut my eyes. The rock and the hand slowly melt into the dark, until only their outlines remain, etched lines across the flickering void. We call it the "afterimage" but it is not afterimage, it is the corruption of the image, the melting away of existence. The end of the world: a slow dissolve.

I blink at the temple of Delphi in Greece and the new world is borne in an act of philosophical crudeness, watching the temple slowly dissolve each time. And we call the perceived objects in our waking states of consciousness solid, and the perceived objects in our dream states of consciousness fluid, ephemeral, discontinuous . . . what seductive power language has over consciousness! I realized, for the first time, that in dreams the so-called "phenomenal images" - the actual

130

(subjective) objects - are not constantly interrupted by gaps in which there is, literally, a black void. It is the objects in our waking states that are in this way gappy; the objects in our dream states are positively surreal in their unbroken presence. I marveled at the crude simplicity of this realization: in dreams we don't blink, meaning that objects in dreams occur without this constant, interruptive flickering, where as in waking states we blink, meaning that there is constant interruption, like a bad computer monitor that goes on and off with such constancy that after a while you simply get used to it.

And then it hit me, how one *can* distinguish dream from waking states! Descartes was wrong. There is a marker and you *can* tell the difference and it's exactly what one's initial intuitions say, except in reverse: vividness of objects! Except dreams are not *as* vivid as waking states. Dreams are far *more* vivid!

My thoughts and attention thus turned back to the objects before me. I was, I now verbally reminded myself, the subject identified as an actual dream body and an actual *dream* mind - the self - and embedded in an actual, dream world. The actual dream world, as such, is an essentially temporal configuration of objects existing of brief durations: temporal duration, as a property of ideas - "extended unextendedness" - can 'extend' only in a *non*abstract, narrative theory, a story, which is not (actual) existence at all but mere possibility, the logical inertia to be but void without the subject; mere virtuality. That hand on the rock is an actual dream hand, an idea; that rock is an actual dream rock; I am an actual dream self, located within this dream body, experiencing the objects

131

that Berkeley and I call trees, the sky, the ruins, perceived as actual objects in the mind from this location (itself a mind-space, that is, a perspectival space with the *I* as the phenomenological vanishing point of appearance) from this first-person point of view. So in these respects everything was exactly as in the dream. Except the world had become a waking dream; in becoming mine, the world became alive.

Yet once again I had to remind myself - or, I should say, it reminded itself in me - that whether sleeping and dreaming or awake and having experience, I am always dreaming. Sometimes I dream with eyes closed. We call that dreaming. Sometimes I dream with eyes open. We call that experience. I had to say it again and again because it was being forgotten even as it was being remembered.

By the dim light of theory it is, physically speaking, as dark inside a brain as inside any mainframe computer. If you opened up my brain at that moment, as I was seeing the temple of Delphi, you would not see any images of pillars, nor the blueness of the sky. Clearly, eyes are not windows. They are, if anything, more like antennas responding to waves of light. But I saw neither waves as such nor neural firings as such; I saw the ancient temple of Delphi, rocks and trees, an open sky. The world that I saw, I firmly believed, was to a certain degree veridical to what ordinarily we would call the physical world. But not perfectly so. Colors, for instance, as philosophers following Galileo would insist, are but "secondary" qualities, existing only in minds and not in things in themselves conceived as physical objects. Whether amongst the psychological phenomena of perception there are any primary qualities at all or whether all phenomena are "secondary" in the sense that they are solely generated by the mind itself, would be a bone of contention between empiricists and idealists. Most empiricists believed in a mind-independent reality consisting either of mathematical objects (as did most practicing physicists, including Newton, Mach and Einstein) or of physical objects (as did some 'physical realist' philosophers none of whom, as far as I know, were practicing physicists). Most idealists believed in a mind-dependent reality, either as a conglomerate of not-mind and mind (as did the various transcendental idealists following Kant), or as pure mind (as did the absolute idealists following Fichte and Hegel). And no matter how you cut experience, what I was looking at - what I was in direct contact with - as an actual (albeit fleeting) dream self projected in and conjoined to an actual (albeit fleeting) dream world, was in theory either a psychological (mental) phenomenon to a certain degree representative of a mind-independent reality, or a psychological (mental) phenomenon nonrepresentative of any other reality. In the former case most philosophers would conceive the psychological (mental) phenomena to be representations of 'reality,' while the latter would conceive them as presentations; still, even in that case, those presentations could themselves in turn be conceived either in merely fictive terms, as a dream or consisting purely of imaginative mind-stuff (as in their various ways did Schopenhauer, Bradley, and Royce[13]), or they could still yet be conceived in realistic terms, as being themselves the dreams that stuff is made of (such as, in their various ways, did the

133

"radical empiricists" William James, Peirce and Dewey[14]). But, in any case, even as I was aware of all of philosophy's verisimilitudes and vicissitudes, as I sat there on that rock experiencing the sunset of my world, it was none other than my own world that thus revealed itself to me. From the tops of the trees waving in the distant wind to the unseen depths of my soul, to the blazing sun hovering just below the horizon and the impenetrable darkness above me and within, all that was actual was *I*, self-consciousness - even as I presented myself to myself in various aspects not as self but other.

Shall I say, I lost myself in myself? Or, I found myself in everything? It matters little what I say. All was lost in the ruins of Delphi – such a place in which to find yourself!

Something mystical was in the air. Every philosopher I've talked to who's been here - even the most hardboiled - has used that very word to describe this place: *mystical*. The weather agrees. The rest of Greece is straw. Here the greenness seems to explain itself in everything, to fall right out of rapidly forming clouds saturated with color.

I went back to my book:

> Life and dreams are leaves of the same book. The systematic reading of this book is real life, but when the reading hours (that is, the day) are over, we often continue idly to turn over the leaves, and read a page here and there without method or connection: often one we have read before, sometimes one that is new to us, but always in the same book. Such an isolated page is indeed out of

connection with the systematic study of the book, but it does not seem so very different when we remember that the whole continuous perusal begins and ends just as abruptly, and may therefore be regarded as merely a larger single page. Thus although individual dreams are distinguished from real life by the fact that they do not fit into that continuity which runs through the whole of experience, and the act of awaking brings this into consciousness, yet that very continuity of experience belongs to real life as its form, and the dream on its part can point to a similar continuity in itself. If, therefore, we consider the question from a point of view external to both, there is no distinct difference in their nature, and we are forced to concede to the poets that life is a long dream.[15]

When it became too dark to read I put the book away. In the purplish gray of dusk, bluer and duller than slate, pink ribbons of light spewed into the afterglow of an electric sunset. I expected at any moment to see one of Zeus's firebolts or the spiral lightning from Apollo's chariot blaze across the silken shadows. The scene was right out of the beginning of *Wizard of Oz*. The treetops trembled in anticipation.

A bolt of lightning flashed from the other side of Parnassus, startling me; half a second later, thunder rolled across the mountain. I put away my things and sat up on the *omphalos*, the navel of the world, and stared up into the gnarled sky full of wind, air, the life breath of consciousness.

The whole Earth was suddenly that rock, the atmosphere its mind. Angry black portentous ink clouds with billows of glowing charcoal swirled across the top of the mountain as if readying to etch these words on the inside of my skull, to initialize the world: *I am.*

I gathered up my rucksack and hurried down the slope toward the temple in search of shelter from the storm. No ceilings anywhere, not even a canopy. It occurred to me to make a run back to the village of Castri but I decided not to let myself be chased away from another night at Philosophy's temple by a mere thunderstorm.

Rain began to fall, warm fat translucent pearls kissing the ancient stone, tickling my toes. *Dream rain,* I thought to myself as the downpour swelled. Watching the patterns of waves weaving across the ruins, I felt the awe of rain: mind *is* rain. Mind is stone. The world is my world. Even if there is another, containing world as conceived in popular science and philosophy – some material, physical, non-perspectival world - the wetness of the rain is a mystery within a mystery and I feel it, here it is: feel the rain. I ran splashing across the puddles, laughing at myself for not having felt properly the wonder of my own being.

The downpour cut unevenly across the slabs, forming gray pools of reflection swaddling the ancient walkways. Crevices of stone turned to rivulets of rain, meanderings of thought. The theater steps became a cascade of ideas. I began twirling, leaping, dancing looselimbed across the ruins. I jumped onto the open stage of what used to be the Theater of Apollo and it made me laugh: welcome, ladies and gentlemen, here we are, live at the Apollo . . .

And then I saw him.

I stopped. Hermes was not due again until noon the next day. Tourists are rare in late September. Rain, even at the height of the season, clears out the main attractions; even the Parthenon in Athens on a rainy day in midsummer becomes deserted. Delphi is far from the beaten path, tourist season was over, it was night, and a thunderstorm was in progress. You absolutely never see the locals at any of the sights, not even in good weather, except as guides or trinket sellers.

He stood halfway between the theater and temple in his nightshirt, the kind they wore centuries ago in Europe and still wear in India. He reminded me of an Indian guru, head slightly bowed against the rain, back erect, his long wild hair slowly swaying, dripping in the downpour. Another bolt struck, a thunderclap right above us, and in the flash I saw his face like a ghost etched in light, silhouetted against the ruins.

It was René Descartes.

ENDNOTES

[1] This is how Josiah Royce translates it; see the discussion of Hegel, and Royce's translation in Daniel Kolak, *Lovers of Wisdom*, Wadsworth 1997, pp. 449-475.

[2] I haven't the space here nor the time to elaborate more fully on the 'five minute theory.' But the proof takes far less time than that; I leave the proof as an exercise.

[3] 90 min = 5400 sec = 5400 sec x 186,284 miles/sec = 1,005,933,600 miles. This is enough of a diameter to encompass the entire solar system as conceived in the (imaginary) theoretical world of physics. Also, it is rather interesting to note that the 'spherical bowl' that was conceived to be the outer limit of the world by the ancients corresponds, by my reckoning, almost perfectly to the correct extension of the world. (I should also add that, contrary to Leibniz's otherwise excellently presented philosophy, monads are big.)

[4] Apperception is a term best understood, for our purposes, as follows. Perception is of course a theoretical term; as was pointed out in earlier chapters, you don't see perceptions, you see objects. (Think of what animals, which don't have a theory of perception, see.) If you have some sort of theory of perception, you then know the sense in which it can be said that your eyes are not windows and that these items presently before your consciousness are, for instance, mental representations of physical objects. Or something like that. The term apperception is intended to distinguish that sort of conception from those items in your consciousness which you take to be items not of the physical but of the mental world: thoughts, emotions, ideas, desires, and so on. Thus any state in which the items in consciousness are taken to be what they are - items not of the physical world but items in the mental world - is an apperception.

[5] See the sections on Fichte, Schelling and Husserl in Daniel Kolak, *From the Presocratics to the Present: A Personal Odyssey*, Mayfield 1998.

[6] See Daniel Kolak, *Wittgenstein's Tractatus*, Mayfield 1998.

⁷ For a discussion of Peirce, Saussure, and related topics see *From the Presocratics to the Present,* op. cit.; here I can only add that *semeion* (plural *semeia*) were used as early as Hippocrates and Parmenides as a synonym for *tekmerion,* variously translated as proof, evidence, and symptom. It was of course Aristotle who distinguished *semeia* from *symbola.* It may not be completely irrelevant to point out that *semeion* was a *medical* symptom, such as "spots." Of course I have no idea what any of this means – I'm 'awake,' sorry.

⁸ See the discussion of Bergson in *From the Presocratics to the Present,* op. cit.

⁹ See Daniel Kolak, "Art and Intentionality," in the *Journal of Aesthetics and Art Criticism,* 48, 1990, pp. 158-162; for one of the finest discussions ever on the relation of art, especially modern art, to philosophy, see Jaakko Hintikka, "Concept as Vision: On the Problem of Representation in Modern Art and in Modern Philosophy," which is Ch. 11 of his very remarkable *The Intentions of Intentionality and Other New Models for Modalities,* Synthese Library/ Volume 90, Dordrecht, Holland: D. Reidel 1975.

¹⁰ See Daniel Kolak, "Quantum Cosmology, the Anthropic Principle, and Why Is There Something Rather Than Nothing?" reprinted in *The Experience of Philosophy,* Kolak & Martin eds., Belmont: Wadsworth 1996, pp. 427-459.

¹¹ Mach, after whom Mach I, Mach II, etc. - the speed of sound - are named, wrote in his classical *Analysis of Sensations* (issued in several key revisions between 1900 and 1913):

> "The superfluity of the role played by the 'thing-in-itself' abruptly dawned upon me. On a bright summer day in the open air, the world with my ego suddenly appeared to me as one coherent mass of sensations, only more strongly coherent in the ego. Although the actual working out of this thought did not occur until a later period, yet this moment was decisive for my whole view. . . . Atoms cannot be perceived by the senses; like all substances they are things of thought."

For further discussion, see the sections on Mach in *Lovers of Wisdom,* op. cit., and *From the Presocratics to the Present,* op. cit., as well as Mach's "Analysis of Sensations," reprinted in *The Mayfield Anthology of Western Philosophy,* Daniel Kolak, ed., Mayfield 1998.

[12]See *The Many Worlds Interpretation of Quantum Mechanics,* B.S. DeWitt and N. Graham (Princeton University Press 1973) and Kolak, "Quantum Cosmology," op. cit. above.

[13] See the relevant discussions in *Preseocratics to the Present* and *Lovers of Wisdom,* op. cit.

[14] Again, the two works mentioned above contain substantial discussions of these philosophers.

[15] Schopenhauer, *The World as Will and Idea,* quoted in Daniel Kolak, *Lovers of Wisdom,* op. cit., and reprinted in *The Mayfield Anthology of Western Philosophy,* op. cit.

FIVE

SELF
AND
OTHER

Everyone is the other, and no one is himself. The they which supplies the answer to the question of the who is nobody.

Martin Heidegger

"I THOUGHT I WAS AWAKE!"

"I thought there was no difference."

We stood face to face, looking not so much *at* each other as for each other. He was about fifty, with the overweight but muscular build of an ex-prizefighter or soldier on furlough. His nose had been broken, perhaps more than once. His shoulder-length hair lay twisted across his face. The jowls below his sunken cheeks, dark bags under his eyes, the ghostly pallor of his skin, made him look slightly deranged.

"How strange," wiping the rain off his brow he stared at me with crazed, wide-open eyes, "to be myself again." He ran his wet hands across my face, like a blind man trying to see by feeling. It made me uncomfortable. "I just dreamt that I was you."

"You think *you're* . . . that I am . . ." But then I thought: what am I even saying? He doesn't think anything. There's no one there inside that apparition looking out. "That's impossible."

"Considering we've now both been the other, yes. I'm not quite sure what to make of this."

He stared at me and I stared back, fascinated by my reflection in his eyes, the image of myself inside the other inside myself.

"I'll tell you what I think, though, what I remember." He wiped the rain from his eyes. "Six months ago I took Pierre Chanut's bad advice and came to Amsterdam to serve the Queen as her personal tutor. It is February now, cold and very bleak, the Queen has learned her lessons and I have caught my death. The year is 1650."

In the distance thunder rolled, a low hollow rumble thickened by the falling rain. He stood with his hands behind his hips, like a solider at ease, and went on:

"All my life I've had a recurring dream. I find myself hiking through a mountain pass on a sweltering summer day in Greece down to the ancient white-hot ruins of Delphi. Always the dream ends on the same discordant note: arriving at the wall of the temple I read the ancient words, *gnothi s'afton,* the noise of cicadas swells and my head empties in the sun so completely I forget who I am and I wake up not knowing, not where nor who nor what I am, only that I am, a maelstrom of unknowing wallowing in the awareness of my own existence, waiting for the world to return me to myself.

"This recurring dream coincides with a singular event in the life of a young man who in relation to me does not exist, who is nowhere in my world, a man not yet born. That man is you. Happenstance?" He shrugged. "For all I know the rapturous rhythm of chaos beating in the wings of cicadas unites us upon a fulcrum of unknowing, a tilt in time through which you slip out of yourself into my dream and I slip out of my dream and tumble into your world, into you.

"Last night I awoke from that dream into another, in which Philosophy enlightened me, a dream that as far as I can tell coincides perfectly with the one into which you tumbled from your waking experience, an intersection of worlds that exchanges and connects us across time and space. Then a third dream, which you would count as second: you dreamt that you woke up into a dream in which you encountered Philosophy no longer as Descartes but as yourself, Kolak. That dream coincides with one in which I dreamt that I was you, a dream in which I remember writing, 'I just awoke from a dream in which I dreamt I was Descartes!' Likewise, my fourth dream coincides with what you regard not as dream but reality: the Italian tourists, Hermes, the taste of kourabiedes, lemon ouzo, the sneezewort, the musings over the *omphalos* stone, your cosmological ruminations . . . I was there, that was my dream, I was you."

He stared at me with a melting look in his roguish eyes. I was speechless. He began walking slowly around me, pacing in a circle, stalking me with his eyes.

"How old are you?"

"Twenty-two."

"You know you look like Mersenne? When we first met. Did you know that?" He coughed, then laughed. "I know your fear," he said, matter-of-factly. "You're relying, hoping, dreaming you've 'really' been 'out there.' Isn't that strange? How we still keep thinking of the world 'out there!' As if dreams were an escape! No, no, it's that world - the waking world - that is the true escape. Shall I tell you how I realized it?" He folded his arms tightly across his chest. "How remarkable, said I to myself, that I should fear in this way for my own existence. I thought my greatest fear was death. But when Philosophy made me realize my 'head' was not the head that I was in and the head that I was in was not my head but my world I became afraid of something far more horrible: my own insubstantiality. Not nothingness, but being no one. Oh, the fear of being not a dead or dying man but a dream man, someone else's ghostly reflection - not someone who shall cease to be but someone who has never been! Not to be a real man, to be a character in someone else's dream, what a feeling of humiliation, of vertigo—"

"I'd like to think that you exist," I said, "I really would. I'd love to believe you are Descartes. But I don't."

"I see." He smiled. "You want to put me on trial, like Socrates? Will you be my Euthyphro? Do I get an apology? Wait," he laughed again, "allow me, like Socrates, to

144

pronounce my own sentence: I think, therefore I am."

"I wish I could believe you," I said. "But how would that be possible? Reincarnation? Possession? How could two men separated by three and a half centuries meet in a dream?"

"I can think of several explanations, none of which I find very plausible. So I can't give you one. I can however prove to you that I exist - that I too am a conscious, thinking being. All you have to do is listen carefully to my argument and answer a few simple questions." He laughed, a deep throaty cackle full of phlegm. "Perhaps if we satisfy the ancient edict to know our selves our God may appear again and reveal how what we know to be true is possible." He coughed and spit into the rain. "My argument is a simple *reductio*. I think you should be able to follow it.. We begin by assuming that I don't exist."

"That should not be difficult."

"Don't be too sure." He grinned, the rain dripping from his long lashes. "What am I, then, to you? An image?"

"In theory, yes. That's not what I see. You're an object."

"Like this rock?" He squatted down and picked up a lose stone from the stage; rolling the rock in his fingers, he examined it. "Do objects talk, converse, ask questions?"

"Not usually."

"Have they ever?"

"No."

"Do objects assert their existence, their identity?"

"Not verbally, no. Not usually."

"What would that be like?" He threw the stone into across orchestra.

"Some arm."

"It's all in the trajectory." It flew in a perfect arc and landed in the uppermost tier, past the colonnade. He would have made a great baseball player. "If a rock began speaking, asserting its existence, what would you think, what would you conclude? Would you not assume this was no mere object but a conscious being, something with a mind, disguised as a rock?"

"Or else that I had lost my mind."

"But you would not conclude that inanimate objects can think, reason – rather, that what looked like an object made of stone was itself, or at least contained, a subject."

"Such evidence would be only circumstantial," I said. "A subject cannot perceive a subject but only objects, like bodies, some of which behave as if animated from within by a subject. So if objects began talking to me – as you now are doing – I would conclude, as I do now, that these were not someone else's thoughts but my own."

"Of course, of course." He rubbed his chin bemusedly. "But the subject does not perceive *itself* as a subject either! Anything the subject perceives is an object - how then does a subject know *any* subject exists, up to and including itself?"

"I see *that* objects are being seen. I think, I feel, I reason. That's how I know."

"The subject perceives itself not because the subject is an object but in virtue of the objects perceived, that's right. When you see that objects are seen from a certain perspective you see yourself without having to perform the impossible act of seeing the unseen seer. Your world is perspectival, it has a center; subjectivity confers itself through the seen fact that

146

objects don't exist for themselves in some absolute realm beyond space and time but for you, identified in the conscious act of seeing. Likewise, your 'internal,' temporal objects – thoughts and feelings – are also perspectival, are they not, except directed not at you but from you . . . " he paused, took a deep breath, and coughed again. "So then what about me? To you I am no mere object but one claiming to be a subject. Moreover, I don't just talk at you like some parrot. This is a dialogue, is it not? You think this is a monologue, that these words are not mine but yours? *Who* then speaks when I speak? You? *Is* it you? Tell me what I will say next, then, can you? You cannot! Speak at the same time as me, in double voice, can you do it? You cannot. If my speech is generated mechanically, or randomly, how does it coordinate with your speech, how does it make sense?"

"But that's true of all the characters in my dreams!"

"Good answer!" He continued circling around me like a duelist on stage - the mindfulness of others not as adversaries but as blocking. "When you wake up from a dream you say to yourself, 'that was only a dream,' secure in the certainty that all the words and actions in the dream were caused by you. Yet, clearly, it is not you, the awake and future self, who remembers having been the other characters whose words you heard, as you heard Philosophy's and now hear mine, from the third person point of view. The 'awake' self is not the one who will have *been* them! Right? For never upon waking do you remember having experienced a dream from any but the 'central' character's point of view. You thus assume there was only one conscious self in your mind, that the other characters

147

are 'dark' inside. Memory – there's the culprit again – insists that all other characters in dreams are mere automata, inanimate objects, empty puppets whose strings are pulled . . . but by whom – by what?"

I began to feel afraid.

"Right now," he went on, "you are not the puppeteer who pulls *my* strings, any more than I am the author of the private thoughts I believe are heard by you from the first person point of view as if from within your own imaginary head. Are you the actor who mouths my words? No! How then can *you* be the cause of my words and actions? How can you explain this meeting as an encounter with yourself, yet go on believing that I am but an 'empty self' not a 'me,' when upon reflection you can see you were not the material cause of my movements nor the mouthing of my words? Since you are not presently writing my side of the dialogue, who is doing it? No one? If *no one* does my thinking and talking, no one who listens and responds to you, you're conversing with a mindless image, a shadow person, a *puppet whose speech is not automatic, nor predictable.* If I am a mindless automaton - of whose mechanisms, I might add, you are completely unaware - how then do these thoughts come to be heard from the third person point of view, experienced by you as what - *voices?* - 'auditory objects?' rather than what they are: subjective experiences, ideas? How is it that 'subjectless objects,' mechanisms that simulate subjectivity, divorced from the subject's consciousness, can generate thoughts, formulate sentences, converse with you without any awareness?

"No, no, wait, I'm not finished. Clearly, you are not the

material cause of these very words you are now hearing, nor of your own - for perhaps in neither case does the subject know how or from where sentences emerge into consciousness - but the formal cause of my speech must, if it is to engage in a dialogue with you, involve a perspective to which your 'output' is coordinated, so that it can be heard, understood, processed. You surmise that for me to be conscious there would have to be representations of a world inside which there is a subject to whom the objects of that phenomenal world are presented. My representations would have to include self-representations, and especially representations of myself as being-appeared-to by things in the world I inhabit. Without such representations my capacity to guide my own higher-order behaviors[1] would be inexplicable! But if I can and do indeed use these representations, then I am a conscious self, like you. For that is what a conscious self is.

"This strikes you, I know, as difficult not only to believe but even to understand. But what is this behavior of mine, involving such an inner perspective, if not a self? If it were not so, this very activity which in your own case you call subjectivity is attainable through purely automatic processes, the apprehension of objects without any subject. Impossible! You see? If I am not to myself in my own world a conscious subject identified as a thinking, perceiving self, with a perspective on my world, there must exist blind forces capable of 'thinking' without consciousness, of asking questions, of causing wonder and distress, of expressing themselves as I am now doing - even of answering questions! - but without anyone being there aware of the words uttered from within

149

oneself. If I do not exist it means thoughts such as these can exist without ever being experienced by anyone from the first person point of view, from the inside. *Could these very words be generated automatically?* Is that possible? How? A thought is language experienced from the first person point of view, is it not? How then should you understand this very speech, these words emerging from automatic, non-conscious processes, given that you hear me respond to you without any direct conscious action on your part? How otherwise than that I am another conscious self could you explain the coherence of this dialogue? Is it a form of automatic writing? I doubt this very much! Indeed, it should make you shudder to think how many characters in your dreams pass the test that in your waking states you would never even think to ask 'waking' selves to meet, most of whom I daresay seem to have barely the self-consciousness of brutes."

Again I was speechless. His argument, made by what I would until having heard it believed without question to be unconscious forces within myself, was an eloquent, intelligent and highly original proof that these were not unconscious forces but purposeful, intentional processes. Even as an imaginary figment of my imagination he was (an indirect, yet ontological) proof of what I had until that dream thought undemonstrable. Even if he didn't exist, Descartes was himself an embodied argument for the truth of what he was saying. Like a mathematical proof, his argument validated itself through the sheer logical force of its own intelligence. Indeed, there was a clear sense in which he passed the Turing test - with flying colors - nearly all my dream characters did![2]

He put his hands on my shoulders. His grip felt solid, real. Aristotle suddenly made sense to me, and the pragmatists, as never before, even behaviorism - provided one properly understood the behavioral action to be taking place within the boundaries of one's own mind. One had to add here the rather disquieting proviso that Aristotle's collapsing of Plato's two worlds into one world is in point of fact not the conceptual explosion of the ideal world from the empirical world so as to allow the one 'real' world to remain standing - surprise! appearance is reality! - but, rather, the conceptual implosion of the external world into the internal world: Plato's two worlds do indeed collapse into one actual world - Aristotle is correct - but the actual world into which both worlds collapse is ideal - Plato too is correct. Two philosophical wrongs do in this case make one metaphysical right.

"There is no longer any question in my mind," I said, taking a step back, "but that you do exist. I don't believe it, I don't *feel* it - I mean, how can I? - but I know it must be true and not just in this dream but in all my dreams. Well, perhaps *know* is too strong a word. But certainly you have given me ample evidence that there are many voices within me, many selves, many worlds, each one with its own conscious subject, an argument that should avail itself to everyone who dreams yet which as far as I know no one has ever made before."

He put a hand back on my shoulder. "How's that book coming?"

"What? Oh. Not very well."

"Don't you write down these dreams?"

"I . . . "

151

"It's no good for me to. My world is not ready for it. Anyway I haven't much time left, I'm afraid. Lucky bastard. You've got your whole life ahead of you! You will remember my argument?"

"What gets down . . . on the page, well, let's just say I find this . . . lucidity, only in my dreams."

"That's how it was with me. It's why I stayed in bed so late." After a pause, he said, "Writing is a matter of trust."

"It's very different in the light of day."

"You lack confidence."

"All I have is confidence."

"You have dreams." He snapped his fingers. "I'll write you a letter! I should be able muster it–"

"What?"

"The only question is where I could hide it or send it that you might one day find it. As long as you didn't show it to anybody, it would be like the book N. gave me–"

"Listen, you are *not* Descartes, all right?" I swallowed hard, suddenly very thirsty amidst all that rain. "Come on, that's crazy, how *could* you be?"

Still gripping my shoulder for support, he narrowed he eyes against the rain. He looked as if he were about to say something, but didn't.

"You've proved that you exist," I said, "but in a dream everyone I meet is myself! Behind your face am I, dreaming I am you, encountering myself in a dream not as self but other. I don't know how or why but that's the only sober explanation. I am I and I am you, why not? If a mind can divide itself into subject and object – as it must to make

152

experience possible – why not into subject and subject? That's what you proved. Not that you are Descartes. That I am more than one self!" I placed my palms on my rain-soaked brow. "I am here, I am I and I am there, I am you. I could of course be mistaken - you might be only an apparition, an empty mask - but you've given me sufficient reason to believe I am there behind your imaginary eyes, masked from myself. I am not one self in one world but many selves in many worlds, the universe within." I licked my lips to get some moisture on my tongue. My throat felt like sandpaper. "Look. You'd love to be Descartes, the father of modern philosophy, a soldier and a duelist, the inventor of analytic philosophy . . . but you're not. You're a young man with too much retsina and ouzo in his veins who has come to Delphi in search of himself, so enchanted by his wild imagination it has run away with him, literally, to cause this hopefully temporary case of multiple personality! Don't ask me to explain how a student like me could become a philosopher like you, I can't, but I know of far stranger cases.[3] All I can tell you is the kind of dissociation that drives the mind into multiple personality disorder can deceive it with all manner of details it has learned but then made itself forget. We're not talking here about some imaginary Cartesian Demon! Let's not drive ourselves mad, shall we? I mean, when I look back at that first dream when I dreamt I was you, in the light of day, yeah, oh yes, I want to play along and I do, swell, what a great book it would make. But not right now when I am in it, no, not when I am in the thick of it, not when it has me in its grip. Hell, not just *that* dream, *any* dream." I shook my head. "You think I don't

153

know the dreamer - whoever, whatever the dreamer is - isn't capable of making me believe, *do* anything? Constantine 'the great' comes to mind, those three little holes in that rock and all the butchering by which the human spirit lives . . ." I wiped the rain from my eyes. "Surely you understand that you cannot possibly be Descartes, that I - you, me, us, whatever – should not think such crazy thoughts!"

I saw my reflection in his pupils as if in a curved mirror. He shook his head and laughed.

"The inquisition," he murmured.

"What?"

"The inquisition!"

"How does–"

"What religion are you?"

"What does that have to do with anything?"

"Catholic?"

"My, uh, my grandparents were. On the one side. On the other too, well, actually, assimilated Jews."

"Christian? How were you raised?"

"I . . . I wasn't."

"Your University . . . run by Jesuits?"

"What? No! I mean . . . look, what are you–"

"All right. I'll tell you a story." He nodded to himself, staring at me with a serious look on his face. "Want to hear a story?"

And suddenly it hit me: what if *I'm* the doppelganger? What if something had indeed gone wrong in me somewhere, and now by proving to me that he existed his dream within a dream had swallowed and now contained my dream, a labyrinth within a labyrinth to hide me from myself, out of the temple of self into the prison of self from which I could no longer emerge? What if *he's* the one who will wake up and emerge from this dream as the (my?) dominant self, the new Head of Mind? Perhaps these dreams were but a mask for the forces of self-possession, containment of selves within selves, a form of insanity in which my own mind conspired against itself, the forging of a new dominant personality based on a false and confabulated identity from whose containment I could not escape and in whose grip I would remain. I might wake up and it would be his mask, not mine, that would present me to myself and to the world, such that when I (he) awoke I would disappear and no longer be myself but, as he still is and I only falsely remember that I was, Descartes. I pictured myself climbing out of the ruins as Descartes, taking the morning bus to Athens, thinking I had died or been reincarnated at the dawn of the third millenium . . .

I wondered what that would be like. I reasoned it would not be anything like death. I would still be there, as in the *Descartes among the ruins* dream, completely dissociated from my 'true' self as if my life had never happened to *me* (though perhaps it never did). I would upon waking think and believe and behave as if I was Descartes - fight some duels, maybe? become a metaphysical soldier of fortune? - with the same feeling of certainty as before, just as he still does, except the world I would wake up in as Descartes would not be Descartes' world but Kolak's world - not the real world (there aren't any), but a world in which my false identity was readily apparent to everyone but myself.

"Well?" He was staring down at his bare feet, playfully diverting the flow of rain across the slab into two streams. "You want to hear this story or not?"

"Sure."

"There are certain delusional states," he said, "which I have heard reported and have myself witnessed." He looked up into the sky, blinking, the rain splashing into his open eyes. "I was once asked by a local magistrate to examine the Madwoman of Alsace. Ever heard of her? No?" A wet grin chiseled itself across his face. "She claimed to be Helen of Troy. Most amazing thing - a peasant woman with no formal education to speak of who claimed to be the daughter of Zeus, sister of the Dioscuri and of Clytemnestra. She insisted her husband was not her husband, that her true husband was Menelaus, Agamemnon's younger brother! Everyone thought it frightfully amusing except her husband, with whom she now refused to sleep on grounds that she did not want to commit adultery!" He chuckled. "That of course is what brought it to the attention of the courts. The thing of it was, by all accounts this woman was completely illiterate! Yet not only could she now read, she spoke fluently in several languages! To prove she was Helen she provided historical details that even many scholars are ignorant of and told us things which seemed impossible for any French peasant to know. Indeed, she wrote and read and conversed with the ability of a high courtesan!" He laughed with an eerie twang, like an instrument thrown out of tune while playing. "You don't like this story? What's the matter?"

"Nothing." I rubbed my face. Trying to remember I felt

156

certain I knew next to nothing about mythology. I realized, of course, that I could be making up everything he said, that I would be able upon waking to check the historical records which no doubt would prove all this to be nothing more than make-believe . . . but still. It wasn't just the thought of Descartes being part of the Inquisition nor the woman herself, but Agamemnon, Dioscurie, Clytemnestra . . . "What did you conclude?"

He seemed rather to collapse than to sit down on the edge of the stage.

"The decision . . . was unanimous." He leaned forward to rub his left foot, as if it had fallen asleep, grimacing in pain. "It was unanimous. It was the 'proof' of her identity that – because it could not be explained - led the court to conclude that she was possessed by a demon." He winced. "She was declared a witch and burned at the stake."

"How could you . . ." I stopped, reminding myself yet again that this was but a dream, that this could not really be Descartes but only, at worst, some part of *me* playing at being him.

Muttering something under his breath he stretched his eyes through the rain and looked right through me, as if focused far away on a different scene.

"I asked her . . ." shaking his head, he giggled nervously, "as an inquisitor it was my right, you see, to ask, it was my duty and my right." Letting go of his foot he dangled his legs over the edge of the stage. "Through the flames, I asked her: *who are you?* She answered me. That's when I thought I knew how right we were to condemn her."

157

"What . . . did she say?"

"She pronounced it slowly, enunciating every syllable. Her eyes, her lips, the skin of her face puffing, boiling, melting, tiny explosions of blood releasing whiffs of pink smoke, I'll never forget that horror . . . she pronounced it so clearly and distinctly . . ."

"What?"

"The forbidden proposition."

"How do you know to say this!"

"You are afraid! You see how you are afraid?" The face staring back at you through the heat as if through running water smiles. "It is you who burns behind my eyes."

"Who taught you to say this? Before you die, tell me."

She spits through the flames into your face and with her hot saliva stinging your eyes she laughs as her hair and eyebrows ignite.

"I must ask you again: Who are you?"

Her face goes up in flames like a paper mask revealing the face that launched a thousand ships and behind that mask yours peeling away revealing yet another and another . . .

"I . . . am . . . you."

"I don't understand."

"She said what you said."

"What are you talking about?"

His head bowed loosely, as if broken. "I am you."

The rain was unmerciful and somehow terrible. It no longer poured but flowed, a deluge from heaven, the noise of existence rattling.

ENDNOTES

[1] To pass the Turing test, for instance.

[2] Alan Turing had proposed a test in which subjects in isolation booths had to determine whether they were communicating with a computer or with a human being. Turing's interpretation was that if the test subjects could not distinguish the minds from the machines, it was time to give up the ghost and regard such machines as minded. Well, in that dream there I was communicating with what common sense said were mere automata. We are thus successfully fooled by our own minds all the time into believing that what are later regarded as 'mere apparitions' are minded, conscious subjects. But then who is fooled? The subject is fooled – by non subjects? Who then does the fooling? Was this another as yet undiscovered form of bizarre self-deception, providing empirical evidence (albeit hopelessly subjective) for the sorts of dissociations that occur in multiple personality disorder? I marveled at the insight even as I was also frightened by it.

[3] One of the strangest is that of Billy Milligan, a high school dropout who was the first person in history found not guilty of major crimes by reason of multiple personality disorder. By the time he was twenty-three and serving time at the Athens mental health Center in Athens, Ohio, doctors had catalogued no less than twenty-four distinct personalities, among them: Arthur, a 22 year old English physicist; Allen, a 18 year old con-man; Tommy, a 16 year old escape artist capable of amazing Houdini-like tricks; Christine, a 3 year old dyslexic English girl; Adalana, a 19 year old lesbian; Samuel, an 18 year old Orthodox Jew; Shawn, a 4 year old deaf boy; Ragen Vadascovinich, a 23 year old Yugoslav who read, wrote and spoke Serbo-Croatian; and "The Teacher," a brilliant and philosophically gifted 26 year old with total recall who helped the doctors integrate (fuse) all the different personalities into one co-conscious entity. See *The Minds of Billy Milligan* by Daniel Keyes, Bantam 1981.

SIX

THE

FORBIDDEN

PROPOSITION

History adds that before or after dying he found himself in the presence of God and told Him: "I who have been so many men in vain want to be one and myself." The voice of the Lord answered from a whirlwind: "Neither am I anyone; I have dreamt the world as you dreamt your work, my Shakespeare, and among the forms in my dream are you, who like myself are many and no one."

Jorge Luis Borges

"WHY WAS IT FORBIDDEN? BY WHOM?"

"The church. Paris, 1270." He stared up at the black clouds that within themselves seemed to be on fire, iridescent gleams of encrimsoned charcoal tumbling across Mt.

Parnassus. "Why?" He smiled at me sullenly. "Maybe because it's true."

I plopped down next to him on the edge of the stage. The puddles of efflorescent rain felt warm and comforting, even as the rain fell still harder.

"Want to hear the rest of the story?"

"Sure."

He looked out through the proscenium across the curved rows of empty seats, the curved orchestra and steps of the theater awash in a cascade of tears.

"The idea that we are all the same person has been passed down through the ages, hidden in the works of Plato and Aristotle and brought to light in the twelfth century by various philosophers, most notably Averroes,[1] who conceived it as an ingenious solution to the problem of reality. Utterly heretical, of course, for it replaces all types of theism with deism. Surely you must have heard of this?"

I swallowed hard. "No. I've . . ."

"What? Go on."

"Well, I have had that thought before."

"Who hasn't! And that life is a dream. At one time or another everyone has such thoughts. Problem is, what does one do with it, right? Crazy thoughts. Go on. Tell me your story first. Then I'll finish mine."

"You fought in several wars, didn't you?"

"I did."

"Why?"

"Because they were there?" He shrugged. "Passion. Adventure." He was biting a cuticle.

"Ever kill anybody?"

"In wars people get killed." The cuticle came off in his teeth. "In duels. Sure."

"It doesn't . . . it didn't bother you?"

"No." He spit out the piece of skin. "It's all a question of tradition. Heritage. Attaining manhood. A ritual." With a sudden disdain in his eyes he sized me up with one stern look. "You've never been? It shows."

"When I was a little boy," I said, "I was very much troubled by the idea of war. I tried to understand the hatreds that drove men to butcher and kill each other--"

"Love," he interrupted. "That's why men kill. Not out of hatred of the other but out of love of self."

"How do you figure?"

"I don't."

"What do you mean?"

"We're flawed," he said, loudly, as if to the rain.

"But it comes down to injustice, doesn't it? If we all had a fair chance, if all of us were given an equal opportunity in the game of life, then there would be no hatred and no war--"

"Bullshit!"

"Look, I was a boy--"

"All right, so you were a boy. Go on."

"I pondered the age-old questions, you know, why does God permit war? Why does God permit injustice? The problem of injustice seemed worse even than the problem of war. I thought about it and thought about it until one day it just hit me, the proverbial flash of inner light in which a solution appeared to me out of the blue. *We are all the same person.*

It was so amazingly simple! There is only one of us. I am you and I am Christ and I am Hitler and I am everybody. There is no injustice in the world. Your suffering is my suffering. The problem of war will end when you realize that in killing me you are only killing yourself."

He burst out laughing.

"I suppose you'd have burned me at the stake?"

"Hardly, my boy, hardly!" He shook his head and when he finally stopped laughing he sighed deeply, wiped his eyes, and gave me a sobering look. "Not unless you *proved* it!"

Again the roll of distant thunder, muffled by the rain. I looked at him, hoping for some glint of irony. In his eyes I saw myself and the whole world drowning.

"Shall I tell you the rest of my story now?"

All I could do was nod.

"It started with the medievals," he said, "a trick question on doctoral exams in philosophy given to students that the Holy See did not want to pass. Is the world real or a work of fiction? You don't want to flunk the exam. But you don't want to be burned for heresy, either!" He laughed. "How would you have answered it?"

"Real."

"Wrong answer! If God is the author of the world, how could the world be real in and of itself? Only God, supreme and uncreated being, could be real in the sense of having an existence that is not dependent or derivative upon another. That answer is pure heresy."

"So the correct answer is fiction?"

"So one might guess. Since the world was created by God

it must ultimately have the same ontological status as a work of fiction, right? Well, what then of morality, of suffering, of redemption . . . justice? They amount to so much nonsense! Only a real being can suffer! If the world is a fiction all the creatures in it are but fictional beings, since because they are created by God their existence is dependent upon another."

"There's no right answer?"

"That's right! If you got that question on your exam the best thing to do was leave it blank and go look for another job! Well, this became such a useful tool that soon variations of the question cropped up in the Islamic world. The dilemma soon began seriously to puzzle various Christian and Islamic commentators. Supposedly, at one time students seeking to overthrow their superiors from both camps would meet secretly in various places, sometimes in the desert; discussions would last days and weeks, a labyrinthine intellectual game full of logical and metaphysical twists and turns.

"I learned about all this from Father Mersenne. As it turned out, one day an unknown student who was given that question answered it! The fundamental idea behind his solution was an attempt to draw a clear and distinct distinction between fiction and reality, in the following sorts of terms. Ask yourself: what is the difference between fiction and reality? The answer must of course be given independently of the terms 'real' and 'fictional,' lest one beg the question. This most promising young fellow took the line that about a work of fiction one can in principle know everything, where as in the case of reality one cannot. The question, 'Is the world and everything and everyone it fiction, or reality?' becomes the question, 'Is the world in principle fully knowable?' If yes, then no. If no, then yes." He paused. "Brilliant line of reasoning, don't you think? I'm sure you see the flaw. Since God by definition knows everything, how can God create a real world, right? You see? God cannot! The young man was commended for his fine work, then promptly executed.

"Ah," he continued, "but word soon got around and a generation or two later there came another attempt to solve the riddle, along the same lines. What if God is the greatest artist, a greater than which cannot be conceived? What would such an artist be like? Well, here another bright young radical thinker developed some tortuous new twists and turns. One very interesting line concerns the question of identity. Which is greater? The artist who fashions a work whose identity is separate from his own, or the artist who out of himself forges a work so integruous and perfect that it is impossible to distinguish between the work and himself? And – here's the most challenging twist - would such a work be understood by the artist? Well I'm sure you can see that there are quagmires here too numerous to mention. But the idea that God to make a real world would have to fashion it not separate from himself but out of himself, a world furthermore that was not understood by its creator and therefore ultimately unknowable and unknown, would in the logically required sense be not fiction but . . . *reality.*"

I stared at him in silence, listening.

"Quite a revolutionary idea," he said, "don't you think? Any being, man or God, conceived either as fully knowable or as an all-knowing being is *therefore* a false and fictional being!

Where as if after some self-reflection and communion with each other it becomes clear to all concerned that we cannot possibly ever know ourselves, we thereby prove that we cannot be works of fiction – and voila! We are real beings in a real world not because we know who we are and what the world is but because we know that we are and the sense in which we also know who, but in the more important sense that we do *not* and *cannot* know *who* we are nor what the world is! Takes you all the way back to Socrates, doesn't it? His love of the unknown, his praise for the wisdom of unknowing."

I realized suddenly what he was getting at. "You're still trying to prove to me that you *really* are Descartes!"

"Hell, I'm trying to prove it to myself."

"Explain to me how a man who lived and died in the seventeenth century and a man living in the twentieth century could be talking to one another like this, in a dream, or in any other way!"

"You tell me!" He gestured with open hands and smiled. "It's your idea!"

"Oh, God." I buried my face in my hands. "This is so crazy. I feel as if I'm possessed or something! I've lost my mind, completely."

"Look, there's a lot more to this story but go on, ask me something. Anything! Ask me things you couldn't possibly know about me–"

"No, no, no, I don't want to play this game with myself, no thank you very much. Not because I don't think it can be played. Because I don't like how such games can come out. You think I want to wake up believing I am you, that I am

Descartes? They'd lock me up! 'Kolak has finally gone over the edge,' they'd say, 'now he thinks he's the reincarnation of René Descartes!' I'm scared enough already by what I know. Listen, when and if I wake up tomorrow morning I'm not spending another minute in this God-damned temple—"

"What happened to 'We're all the same person?'"

"I was twelve years old!"

"You mean, you were only making a philosophical point!" He laughed. "Shall I finish my story?"

"Finish your story!"

"What do you think happened to that second student?"

"Burned at the stake, no doubt."

"Wrong! Wrong religion." Chuckling, he shook his head. "His name was Ibn Rushd. You know him as Averroes. He passed his exams and went on to argue that the world is the living mind of God. What is true here in this dream and what you thought was true when you were twelve years old Averroes claimed is true of everyone everywhere. God is the dreamer. God is everyone. The identity of God and the world is mirrored in the world by the numerical identity of all conscious beings. All souls are one soul, the soul of God, who in order to make the world real must make a labyrinth which even God cannot solve, you see? The world and each life breath of consciousness within us becomes unknowable and unknown . . . *and therefore real.* How could the Islamic theologians have allowed this?" Descartes grinned. "Because Averroes constructed his proof using the Aristotelian distinction between the active and passive intellect to explain what is the source of the one and the many. Very, very clever, don't you see, to use not an Islamic thinker yet one universally well regarded at the time; they called Aristotle *the* philosopher." He sighed. "The same things aren't known by all minds even though they are the same consciousness in action because the passive intellect differentiates us - you are over there seeing and thinking your perceptions and thoughts, I am over here seeing and thinking mine. The passive intellect is not immortal. It dies. The active intellect, consciousness - *nous* - is not only immortal but everywhere identical, the subject of each and every world, one being manifested in all of us - like an actor who unbeknownst to himself plays simultaneously all parts on the stage of the world."

"You actually believe this?"

"I must say I never found this view nearly as plausible as some philosophers at the University of Paris did. Averroes' argument that consciousness within each individual human being is everywhere identical I found most obscure. But that's the idea. *Your* idea. Like all ideas, it has a history." He held up his hands. "It's a great story, isn't it? The traitor and the hero are the same man. The murderer murders himself. The victim flees from himself. All armies on all sides fight enemies who are themselves. God and Devil, sinner and saint, one being is all beings, the dreamer who dreams all dreams." His lips quivered into a smile.

"So then what happened?"

"The history is extremely convoluted. I don't know the whole story. During the time that Islamic theologians tried to reinterpret their understanding of Greek philosophy away from Averroes' monopsychism - and, finding there were good

169

arguments for it, soon banned it - the idea was much discussed within Christendom as a Muslim heresy, you know, the enemy of my enemy . . . anyway, it excited the attention of secular thinkers in northern Europe and developed a large following in the thirteenth century . . . surely as a philosophy student you've heard *some* of this before?"

I shook my head. "No, but when I wake up–"

"You'll become a true lover of books, a real philosopher!" He laughed. "Christian theologians, notably St. Albert and St. Thomas, saw in *I am you* the end of all social order and orthodox institutions, not just of Islam but of Christianity as well. Unlike their Islamic counterparts, they united as a front against the Averroists by proclaiming monopsychism to be a Christian heresy as well. In 1270 the church formally banned its utterance – even to say *I am you* was punishable by death – along with a slew of other taboos, the infamous List of Forbidden Propositions - the same year in which Thomas Aquinas published *On the Unity of the Intellect: Against the Averroists*. Ever read it?"

"I've heard of it," I lied.

"Well, in any case," he said, shaking his head sardonically, *"I am you* has as far as I know the unique distinction of having been banned by two opposing and antithetical religions. Although a few Averroists continued teaching in secret the idea was repressed from mainstream western thought, apparently," he threw me a look of consternation, "quite successfully."

We sat for what seemed a long time, silent, watching the rain pouring down the pillars and walls.

170

"But if it were true that we are all the same person," I said, "wouldn't everybody already know it, believe it? Why would you or I or anyone else have to say it, argue for it? Why not let it come to everyone, not from one self to another, but on its own?"

"As it would to a child, you mean – by direct revelation?" His eyes darkened and his face grew hard and stern. "Perhaps the church was right." He raised his eyebrows, the rain streaming down his face. "Perhaps the teaching should be forbidden."

"But it isn't true, it can't be! It's an impossible idea, silly and childish, utterly absurd."

Leaning forward on his elbows, looking at his large hands, his skin shimmering in the downpour, he examined his palms and fingers as if trying on gloves. "Look, why did you believe in that earlier dream that you were not – and could not be – anyone other than Descartes? Why would you then have considered it as absurd to suppose that you are a young man living in the 20th century named Daniel Kolak? Because you did not then remember Kolak! You see what we have learned here?" He turned his face to me, his eyes transfixed, the rain dripping sideways off his brow. "Our method of self-knowledge is false. On the basis of who we think we are we think we know who we are not. But how do we know we are not Socrates, Plato . . . Mersenne, Helen of Troy, or anyone and everyone else who has ever existed? We think we are not them because we don't remember having been them. As if memory were a metaphysical boundary between identity and nonidentity." His eyes lit up as if fulminated from within by an invisible fire, his voice still mellow and soft. "Because we have not anyone else's memories we believe we are not them; we think we are correct, that we are no one else other than who we are. But even if we are correct and our beliefs are true it is for the wrong reason and that is what we cannot see, not ever, because we are intoxicated by our identification with memory, blinded by our own presence in the world." He blinked, the drops rolled off his lashes, and stared at me through the slanting rain. "Each self is obscured from all the others by the subject as surely as the noonday sun obscures the moon and stars."

I buried my face in my hands to feel the cool repose of the dark, the darkness within the darkness within me made by the appearance of covering my nonexistent eyes with my dream hands . . . it made me laugh even as I felt in my own infinite emptiness the fearful amorphous presence of boundless existence. *Here is my true face, I have found you in the dark and empty inner mirror of dreams, this darkness in myself, knower unknown, seer unseen, the unknowing presence illuminating this and every other world, the face of no one who is everyone . . .*

Descartes stood up and offered me his hand. I took it.

The rhythm of the rain splattering across the ruins had the steady staccato of fingertips tapping at keys, the music of existence falling into consciousness. The black clouds deepened across the top of Mt. Parnassus. The ruins glistened in the frosty darkness, a wet and surreal sheen.

We stood next to each other on the stage looking out into the pouring rain. I looked at him, the rain diverting itself into

172

his sorrowful smile, this wet man with his eyes welling up, his hair matted down across his face, his fiery eyes aglow with an intensity I had seen only in the dark glow of Philosophy's pupils. Such a powerful thing passed between us at that moment, utterly ineffable, that I would only venture to say it was something primordial - a thing between two men, or one man, or none I cannot say, for we both were but dream men - yet utterly sacrosanct. A sense of timelessness, perhaps, that the trendy verisimilitudes of intellectual and spiritual fashions clothe in white labcoats and black robes but which Philosophy's arguments unveil in the tumultuous silence of a dream. In whispers to one's self, numinous and deep. In the sound of rain, washing across the ruins.

SEVEN

DEATH

AND

AWAKENING

The philosophical I is not the human being, not the human body, nor the human soul with which psychology deals. The philosophical self is the metaphysical subject, the boundary – nowhere in the world.

                                        Ludwig Wittgenstein

LIGHTNING STRUCK THE TOP OF MT. Parnassus; the bolt ignited across the crown of pines and spread upward and downward, sputtering, obliterating everything in its path. The stars above and the earth below

174

vanished into the imploding maelstrom.

Fade to black. Dissolve to nothing. Then fade the nothing out.

"Monsieur Descartes? Monsieur Descartes?"

I sat up in the darkness and screamed. The nothing nothinged itself. The scream died in my throat.

Fade in. The crisp snapping sound of logs crackling, a flickering amber light, shadows on the wall, my friendly familiars. The chamber felt cold even though across the room in the fireplace the fire blazed. In my throat the swelling thirst felt like a wound from a sword. With trembling fingers I reached the silver bell on the night table. The bell rolled and fell to the floor clanging across the elephant, the zebra, the tiger, the monkey, the python, ridiculous marble inlays carved into the maroon and ivory tiles. I collapsed back into my drenched pillow.

"Monsieur Descartes?"

It was the chambermaid, her robe half open. I tried to speak but my voice was a growl. She started wiping my forehead with a towel, then propped me up with pillows. The crushing pain, now in my chest, shivered through me. The bed shook.

"The letter," I managed to whisper through gritted teeth, gasping for breath.

Holding me at arms length she looked away. I inhaled her clean unperfumed pungency, strong and fresh, like earth. Her arms were strong. She sobbed; she couldn't hold me still.

"Why am I shaking like this?"

"I don't know, sir."

"The letter," I said, "I want . . . to finish . . . my letter."

"Try to rest, Monsieur. You must."

"That's what the grave is for."

"Don't–"

"My letter, now! Please!"

She pulled the page from my hand and began reading:

"February 11, 1650:

Dear Marin,

I just woke up from a . . ."

Suddenly and without another word she folded up the bloated page and stuffed it between her breasts, then just as quickly crossed herself. It made me laugh, the stupidity of her fear no less so than the stupidity of my trying even on my deathbed to have the last word. Philosophy was right: I was a man of letters, truly, up to the very end

"Why won't you let me finish my letter?"

"To whom is it written! The doctor says–"

"The doctor is an idiot."

"I'm sorry, Monsieur." Crying, she tried to comfort me. "I'm sorry." She brought me water. "I can't help it–"

"It's all right. I am an idiot too."

"This is the devil's work–"

"I'm not angry, please."

She went and stoked the fire, poking through the ashes as if looking for something. Suddenly she reached into the flames and brought out a handful of coals. She turned. It was Helen, her face ablaze.

"What do you want from me!"

Grinning she pulled her hand from the flames, her hand was on fire, I closed my eyes.

"Here, drink."

"This isn't real."

"Drink it."

I shut my mouth and eyes so I wouldn't scream, I could feel the hot coals being forced through my lips . . . I opened my eyes, her face was in flames, she was putting cinders between my lips . . .

"Oh, Jesus."

"Open up, sir. I made you some tea."

I swallowed. It was the maid. When she quietly asked me if she could do anything else for me I quietly told her to leave the room.

I stared at the fire. The pain, as it had now for days come and gone, cleared enough to let me breathe provided I stayed like that and did not move. The body, in its dying, seems perpetually to be searching for a balanced stillness where it can perch a moment and rest before it gets another thrashing, to gather what rest it can before the next, perhaps final, onslaught. And that pain, on my left side, it was back, unbearable . . .

How in the end the body clings to life! It battles for every breath. It does not surrender. And the mind? Death is the before you were born and the infinity of moments preceding it; death is the moment after you shall die and the infinity of moments that will follow; death is within and below you at the most minuscule level of your being; death is above you in the moon and sun and stars. Death is not nothing. Death is everywhere, in everything. Life is but a mere and transparent membrane of in-betweens, a tiny string of momentary dreams beaded by death. Death is the string, the black knit of identity. Death is in everything, death is outside everything, death almost is everything. It is you who is almost but not quite nothing, the always vanishing but never extinguished spark in the ever elusive middle, the breath at the center of a horizonless world. You are a tiny dot of pulsating awareness surrounded by nothing even beyond which there is only you. Death is the empty iris of the mind's eye, the imaginary hole through which your world exists, each one another dream.

And what is the mind at this frantic moment doing? Searching, I noted, for something to take along on its journey into the undiscovered country. I want something to take upstairs, I heard life's voice say, clingy and irrational, hopeless without a story. In that twilight moment of desperate lucidity my own mind asked itself: can a man be more certain than you are at this moment that you are you? And I answered: No. It is this that the dying soul seeks to carry forth into the unknown: the certainty that it is someone, that one, when the truth is that anyone at all will do. The awareness of one's own fleeting existence echoing through some future as yet unlived time: personal identity thrown impersonally forth into an abyss of unknowing. When not intellectualized as an abstract concept personal identity in this way becomes the amorphous self-consciousness in the invisibly burning presence behind your imaginary eyes. It is this that does not want to be forgotten as you move across the threshold from the ending of one dream and signaling already the beginning of another. In

178

that lucid moment I realized, too, that I was a blank fact, as empty and certain as a tautology, no less necessary, full of everything: I am I. Even if I am not Descartes and all this, too, is but a dream dreamt by someone else, I am then that other someone, that one, I am not nothing: I am the hollow nothing, in everything, I am you.

With a sudden jolt lightning struck the chamber, shattering the windows, shooting inward through the imploding glass, tongues of fire reaching in to me . . .

"Monsieur Descartes? Monsieur Descartes!"

I forced my eyes open. It was the doctor with the chambermaid behind him. Too weak to speak, too much in pain to move, I lay limply as they tended to my fever, changing my nightshirt, wiping me down with cool water.

Shadows were taking over the room. My eyes closed as if with a will of their own. I listened to the fire, listening when you can no longer see the light, footsteps shuffling across the floor, your heart, the breath. I remembered as a boy lying asleep at night watching the dancing shadows on the ceiling, terrified of the dark and all it needed was my father to peek in but no one ever did and suddenly no breath, you open your eyes, a swirl of silhouettes, mouth agape, nostrils flaring . . . breath goes in. It stays, empties itself. Burned up, it becomes a black hole within you. Get out! The blackness swells in to swallow you. On your deathbed it is not mind that everything is but body; nothing is ideal, everything is concrete, even breath by which the sluggish machinery struggles to ignite itself back into existence. I can't breathe. I can't . . . enter. I'm on the outside reaching in, I am breath . . .

I felt a hand on me. I opened my eyes. It was him. He stood next to the bed, holding my hand, a somber smile upon his face.

"You?" I said. "I thought . . . what are you doing here?"

"Same as you. Dreaming."

"I told her I was no Boethius. And lucky Jesus! At least he was crucified. I die of a cold. Just don't expect me to die like Socrates–"

"You're raving, Monsieur."

I blinked; it was the doctor.

"He looks like Marin."

"Who does sir? Can you hear me, Monsieur?"

"Unfortunately."

"Do you want a priest?"

I closed my eyes. "Those false alarms."

"The Queen keeps asking to see you," he said. "I must continue to forbid it."

"It's what she pays you for."

"She fears for your soul, Monsieur - if you do not see a priest . . ."

I tried to laugh; a gurgle came out. "Where's Helen?"

"Please, Monsieur."

"The doctor," said the maid, taking my hand, "listen, to the doctor, do you want your soul to wander the Earth–"

"Shut up, woman!" the doctor shouted, pushing her away.

"He is Catholic. He must see a priest. In the village they fear for him and for the Queen, they say he communes with the devil–"

"Never mind about his soul! Take care of the man." He turned back to me. "Anything I can do?"

I looked at him. Ugly man. "Ask the witch what she did with my letter."

He looked away, at the chambermaid.

"I said, where is my letter!"

"Sir. Please."

"Where is it!"

He said, "Sir, Father Mersenne, I am sure you will remember when you are more lucid, your friend has been dead for two years."

"Yes, I . . . oh, damn, is that the name . . . it's not his name. Shit! I can't remember his name."

"*Whose* name, sir?"

"Mine."

"Sir, you're not making any sense–"

"Will you please just write down what I say–I am no one! Tell them. I am everyone. Say that. Write it down."

"Monsieur, I beseech and implore you." He shook his head. "As your doctor I must tend not only to your body but to your mind as well, which most certainly includes your reputation. I must in your final hours protect you from yourself."

"Tonight when I kiss death on the lips," I said, "I will stick my tongue down her throat–"

"In the morning," he smiled, "another surgeon is coming."

"Is he less ugly?"

"You are a remarkable man, Monsieur. Your life has been most extraordinary . . ."

I closed my eyes.

"Never mind, I was merely trying to engage but I see it troubles you . . . I am sorry, can you sleep?"

I nodded. He gave me some medicine, which I took.

"This will help you sleep."

"Will it help me dream?"

"You, Monsieur, are quite the expert on that. Try to rest, please? Monsieur? What is it, Monsieur?"

I was pointing at the figure standing in the doorway.

"It's him," I managed to whisper. "My God. It's him."

"Who, Monsieur?" The doctor turned. "There is no one there."

When again I looked I was gone.

Epilog:

I
THINK
THEREFORE
I
AM
WHO?

And if he left off dreaming about you . . .

Lewis Carroll

I AM. I EXIST. I AM NOT DEAD. I HAVE DIED, I
am Descartes, I am dead. I am not Descartes. I am Kolak. I

am not Kolak. Dying I am reborn. I am not I. I am you.

I never woke up at Delphi. I have never been to Delphi. I am asleep at Delphi still.

Some nights I wake up in terror, fearing that I am neither Descartes nor Kolak but Socrates, that I have drunk the hemlock and that the whole history of philosophy is not a series of footnotes to my author but a series of dreams from which I cannot wake except into other dreams, that I have never left the cave; other nights, I dream that I am no one.

Perhaps I am already in the grave. Or perhaps I will meet myself momentarily in your mirror. But even if I see myself in your eyes still I know I will again as I must forget who I am.

Democritus tore out his eyes in joyous despair to see what cannot be seen. I blind myself so you can see.

Mirrors are the darkest glass in Plato's cave.